olutionary Witness
and
Nobody Here But Us Chickens

Revolutionary Witness, a series of four monologues, was
commissioned by BBC TV as part of their celebrations for
the bicentenary of the French Revolution in July 1989.
Simon Callow played The Patriot, Alfred Molina The
Butcher, Alan Rickman The Preacher and Janet Suzman
The Amazon.

Nobody Here But Us Chickens was commissioned by
Channel 4 and first broadcast in September 1989. The title
play is about two men who believe they are chickens; *More
Than A Touch Of Zen* shows how two supremely ill-equipped
pupils try to learn judo. *Not As Bad As They Seem* is a sexual
farce with a difference.

Peter Barnes is a writer and director whose work includes
The Ruling Class, Nottingham and Piccadilly Theatre,
London (1969); **Leonardo's Last Supper** and **Noonday
Demons**, Open Space Theatre (1969); **Lulu**, Nottingham
Playhouse (1970); **The Bewitched**, Royal Shakespeare
Company at the Aldwych Theatre, London (1974);
Laughter!, Royal Court Theatre, London and **Red Noses**,
Royal Shakespeare Company at the Barbican, London
(1985). He has also written numerous films and radio plays
and has adapted and edited extensively for the theatre.

Peter Barnes

Revolutionary Witness
and
Nobody Here But Us Chickens

METHUEN DRAMA

First published in 1989 by Methuen Drama, Michelin House, 81
Fulham Road, London SW3 6RB and distributed in the United
States by HEB Inc., 70 Court Street, Portsmouth, New Hampshire
03801

A CIP catalogue record for this book may be obtained from the
British Library.

ISBN 0-413-62170-7

Typeset by ↖ Tek Art Ltd, Croydon, Surrey

Printed and bound in Great Britain by
Cox & Wyman Ltd, Cardiff Road, Reading

Caution

Contents

Revolutionary Witness

Author's Note

Most of history is still written from the view from the top. This is history from below. These four, obscure characters are always in the background – one of the crowd, part of the mob. But they speak more directly to us than King Louis, Robespierre or Danton ever could. It is always difficult to feel any human kinship with leaders or politicians, past and present.

These monologues – the four seasons of revolution, Spring, Summer, Autumn, Winter – are studies in the way ordinary – extraordinary people make sense of the world and try to change it. They are not studies of typical revolutionaries for I do not believe there is such a thing as a typical revolutionary or a typical reactionary bourgeois for that matter. These people are not average but they make points of entry into the French Revolutionary period. At the same time they have something to say about the present, where we live under another regime of privilege and injustice but without the prospect of the Bastille falling and the world turning upside down.

Peter Barnes 1989

Revolutionary Witness was first broadcast by BBC TV in July 1989 with the following cast:

The Patriot	Simon Callow
The Butcher	Alfred Molina
The Preacher	Alan Rickman
The Amazon	Janet Suzman

Produced by Margaret Windhan Heffernan
Directed by Jonathon Dent

I

THE PATRIOT

Palloy *stands in front of a skeleton, balls and chains, and a set of manacles. All have price tags and are hanging on a wall below the words 'Live Free Or Die'.*

On either side of **Palloy** *are neat piles of stones of various shapes and sizes, each marked with a price in white chalk. Elegantly displayed amongst the stones are various expensive gift-cases containing medals, pieces of wood and model replicas of the Bastille. All are priced. The whole effect is of a superior window display.*

Palloy (*singing*). 'Patriot Palloy, Patriot Palloy, on the sacred altar of Liberty Laid his heart and his genius for all to see. / His heart he gave to his country. / His genius to his immortality. / Patriot Palloy, Patriot Palloy.' That's me, Citizens. Patriot, Entrepreneur, Architect, Songwriter, Soldier, Philosopher, Revolutionary and all round good fellow – Patrius Franciscus Palloy, the Messiah of Liberty. My card . . . (*He flicks out a card.*) No name on it, no name needed. Only the image of the Bastille, a sword, scythe and tricolor. That's enough to tell you it's Patriot Palloy himself who welcomes you to the grand opening of Palloy's Emporium, 20, Rue des Fosses, St Bernard, Paris, the exclusive purveyor of authentic souvenirs of the Revolution.

Citizens, Brothers, Fellow Republicans, history is nothing but decoration. Here it's for sale. These real Bastille stones washed clean by the blood of the oppressed and crying out 'Buy me! Buy me!' are precious mementoes of the most glorious day in the history of the world, July 14th 1789 when we suddenly walked light with our feet barely touching the ground.

Why should the old religion have the monopoly of holy relics? What're Moses' bones compared to the bones of an unknown never-to-be-named prisoner, found hanging in the deepest Bastille dungeon, dead white and stinking? These are our holy things now, and more precious far, than the nails from the True Cross – and more authentic. They may not cure diseases of the flesh but watch 'em work their wonders on diseases of the spirit, for they banish bitterness and despair in an instant and give true believers radiant hope that centuries of oppression can be overcome. They

are carriers of light, light not from above but from
ourselves.

I've elected my Apostles to transport two hundred and forty
six cases of Revolutionary relics throughout the provinces.
Each Apostle will give a speech in the various provincial
capitals before handing them over to agents who will sell
them on commission. The old Church has been making
money out of their faith for centuries, now it's our turn.
Human beings find it difficult to value anything, even
Liberty, unless they've paid for it. I think you'll find the new
religion less expensive than the old. Just look at the prices.

I'm not ashamed to admit I'm here to spread the good word
– and make a profit too. I learnt that from my father,
Georges Palloy. Just before he died he ordered me to bury
him with his hand left sticking up out of his grave in case
somebody passed with something he could grab. He could've
been a great man but he lived the life of a cockroach. We all
did in the bad days. My mother wore herself out lighting
other people's candles. Poverty makes beautiful women ugly.
We suffocated under tons of bird droppings, now we can
soar.

Some say we're building a new aristocracy on the ruins of
the old. We are, but it isn't a permanent class of vermin like
the old. It's an aristocracy of trade which changes daily like
the waves of the sea. Trade is the new force in the world. It
displaces hereditary privilege and physical strength, calling
forth powers that were left to rot in the former age.

You see how we've all become philosophers now? I know
there's no rational basis for revolutionary optimism given
our lifelong weaknesses and selfishness. Either mankind falls
back into darkness or else the Revolution succeeds and
creates something new. This Revolution of ours isn't a short
moment in which one power overthrows another but a long
moment in which power is dismantled to bring into
existence a society in which all powers will be done away
with because every individual has full power over
themselves. These stones will help build that society and
make it strong. And any one of you can be part of it for as
little as ten francs.

I'm selling the Revolution to the world. These stones, bones and manacles give everyone a taste of it, as they sit in warm corners. The New Americas are already my best customers. General Washington ordered a large stone, Citizens Jefferson and Hamilton splinters from a Bastille beam. Flanders, Italy and Austria all want to buy. There's a demand from every country, except England. The English aren't interested in Liberty: never have been. They're the most servile collection of flunkies left at large in Europe. They tried Revolution once. Killed a King even and took their first steps to freedom. But the experience was too much for 'em. They soon flopped back on their knees and they'll never get up. That's why they're fighting us now out of the shame for their long cowardice. They can't win. (*Singing.*) 'Our enemies we shatter / Their forces we scatter. / Our glory complete. / The sight of a free people. / No retreat, no retreat.' My own composition. Words and music. Two sous a sheet. You can buy copies on your way out. There's a full selection on display in the other room.

It's a patriotic song from a patriot. In France we can be patriotic without wanting to vomit. France is the Revolution and if we're for the Revolution, we're for France. So why not buy yourself a song and better still a medal, Citizens, and show the world you're a patriot? These medals inscribed with the motto 'Liberty or Death' are made from the chains of the Bastille drawbridge, chains we have the courage to break. In the old days such medals could only be bought by the rich. Ordinary people like us had to die gloriously on some forgotten battlefield before we were given one. Now they're on sale to all at ten francs each, whilst stocks last. Who's to say in years to come, they'll be less valuable than the starry ornaments pinned on the pidgeon chest of some Court toady?

One thing is certain, you can take your place at the 'Feast of Reason' or the 'Feast of the Supreme Being' wearing your medals with pride. And it is important, Citizens, we attend our Festivals and Feast days fully rigged.

When I came to stage the 'Feast of the Supreme Being' in my home section of Sceaux I knew how to do it right. We started early with the sun coming up over the rim, new day, new hope and the town crier calling each citizen to pray to the God of their choice in their own manner. All the houses were decorated with flowers and we came out into the streets and embraced each other, swearing our hatred of tyranny and love of friendship. Thousands of people parading through the town square dancing the *'ronde national'* and singing the *'ça ira'*. Thousands of people and no police. I armed the marshals with sheaves of wheat instead of clubs and bayonets. A free people have not need of force to restrain themselves.

It was all a brilliant success. But success evokes enemies, especially in these times. Just as the Republic has its foes I have mine and they are the same – the envious, the weak and the fearful!

They saw their chance with the Tuileries fire. Some of you look puzzled. You don't remember. I never tire of telling the story because it illustrates even someone, such as I, whose spotless patriotism is known countrywide, is still vulnerable.

The Tuileries caught fire and I organized the team to put out the blaze and restore any buildings left standing. For that I was accused by the Minister of the Interior, the infamous Citizen Rolland, of not paying my workers and removing certain unclaimed items from the Tuileries. Oh Liberty, forever smeared and foul-mouthed had a friendly hand to tighten round your throat!

My dear wife pointed out all the workers had indeed been paid by the money raised by selling the missing items. How else? These are hard times and we must improvize. But the Minister wouldn't listen. He had a mind of his own which was probably his greatest weakness. We all live on the razor-edge of luck, Citizens, and I was clapped in prison and the case taken to the National Assembly. My wife and I selected our youngest daughter Simone to defend me.

She was seventeen, wild as a fawn, sweet as maple syrup, as beautiful in the face as any angel could be. She stood in the front of the National Assembly in the pure white robes of

Liberty crying 'Patriot Palloy is innocent! My dearest Papa is without reproach! Long live Liberty, Equality and Fraternity!' And then she sang the 'Marseillaise'. The whole Assembly joined in, crying and singing and that grease-spot of history, Citizen Rolland, was lucky to escape with nothing worse than a broken arm and pelvis.

That bright figure of a girl defending her father won all hearts to the truth. Of course it helped she was young and beautiful and the delegates were all Frenchmen. But images are more important than words. Simone clad in white reminded them of my innocence just as these stones and beams, soaked in martyrs' blood, will remind you and your children of the Revolution. Through the years memories will fade and even those of us who lived through it all will wonder if it happened. My mementoes will be permanent proof it did.

Even now when it's still so near, I sometimes wonder if it was all a glorious dream. But I look on these speaking stones and I know I'm there again, on that first day, July 14th '89. I touch them, and the current of history passes through my fingers. I tremble and live that glorious day again.

Some say I'm not on the official list of those who took the Bastille. *Ha*! They say there was a Paillot and a Pallet but no Palloy – *ha*! So much for *facts*! That's what's wrong with dust-dry historians, they're only concerned with facts. Because it isn't written down they'll say it didn't happen. It happened. Palloy was there. I'm still there. I'll always be there.

Bread had just risen to fourteen and a half sous and the morning sun shone clear in a new sky as thousands of us marched on the clapped-out barracks of the Invalides all cockade bright with drums, fifes, tin whistles, shouts and cries. That great river of humanity swept up over the parapet to come face to face with a great cannon primed ready to blow us all to pieces. But Governor Besenval didn't fire. He was frightened of damaging a house he owned nearby. Dust-dry historians won't understand that those are the hidden hinges of history.

We took the Invalides, captured thirty thousand muskets but no powder or shot. But our blood was primed and we roared 'To the Bastille! To the Bastille!', Tens of thousands of us were on the march, artisans, workers, joiners, builders, carpenters, dressmakers, locksmiths, nailsmiths, blacksmiths, the oldest was Citizen Crétaine aged seventy two and the youngest little Lavalee, all of eight. But our leaders weren't there. Danton and Desmouline arrived after it was all over. It's when leaders usually arrive. It's what makes them leaders.

I remember the watchmaker, Humbert, was the first to climb one of the Bastille towers and then Citizen Davanne and Denain managed to let down the drawbridge and so we flooded across. 'To the Bastille! To the Bastille!' Governor Launey opened one of the outer gates and let us into the great courtyard. When it was packed tight the honourable Governor opened fire on us with his troops. Volley after volley cut us down. Suddenly there was blood and death all around but we didn't flee or turn tail. We preferred to be killed, realizing at last it's less hard than dying. That was the turning point. We stood our ground and died there. But I wonder if we would have if it had started to rain. We'd probably have gone off home, Bastille or no Bastille, and would never have seized the chance to live free. How many times has bad weather changed the world?

Anyway we stayed and fought. Courage grows by daring, fear by delay. We set fire to a Santerre brewery cart filled with straw so the smoke filled the courtyard and the troops couldn't see us. Then reinforcements arrived with guns and cannon and mortar, and we could now fight back. There was confusion and disorder in the smoke and the dying, the screams and the groans and cries, but there was also true glory. Because you see, every man there was his own leader, and he followed his own impulses. Most of us had never handled a gun in our lives yet soldiers on the ramparts swore they'd never been under such disciplined musket fire; they couldn't raise their head above the parapets. We were no longer a mob but a free people fighting for life and liberty.

Suddenly it was over. The Swiss Guards refused to go on and the Governor surrendered. As he was taken away screaming 'Kill me! Kill me!' he accidentally kicked Desnot the baker straight in the privates, *ooohh, ahh*! Old Desnot collapsed clutching himself and groaning 'I'm done'. And some hot-heads stabbed the Governor, shot him six times and cut off his head. Pity, you could say he lost his head by kicking Desnot in exactly the wrong part of his anatomy. Anywhere else he might've survived.

But I was too busy to worry about Governor Launy. People were already stripping the Bastille bare. Taking anything that was takeable, free of charge. Looting was rampant. I immediately got it organized. The National Assembly made it official. That's how I came to have the sole rights to dismantle the Bastille. I think I've done my duty there, Citizens, as this Emporium demonstrates.

But in truth I never saw my job as merely tearing down tyranny's walls but also of building Liberty's ramparts. My dream is to build a Monument to the Glory of Liberty on that site. Naturally I've designed it all myself. There'll be houses, shops, gardens, covered walks, fountains, long straight streets. The Street of Victory, the Street of Legality, the Streets of Equality, Abundance and Renewal. Dream streets, dream gardens and fountains, but we'll make them real. There'll come days that will be short and we'll sleep long but now, it's up and doing! Buy my goods, Citizens, buy 'em and then join me in building the future. It won't be a Utopia of cloudless skies but it will be better. Instead of Bastille darkness we'll have Palloy light. Up and doing, Citizens! Up and doing! Can't you feel the joy of living a life that sings! *Aeeeee*. (*Singing and dancing*.) 'Liberty is dear to us, Happiness is near to us / Joyfully appear to us / It's all clear to us / Up and doing Citizens. / Up and doing! . . .'
Don't forget, Citizens, individually signed copies of this speech can be obtained on your way out, priced three sous. History is yours for less than a glass of Spanish wine . . . (*Singing*.) 'Liberty is dear to us / Happiness is near to us / Up and doing, Citizens / Up and doing!'

II

THE BUTCHER

The National Assembly is in session. **Robert Sauveur** *stands on a small rostrum in a bloodstained leather apron, a meat cleaver and knife stuck in his belt. His sleeves are rolled up and his arms are flecked with blood. A huge tricolour flag covers the wall behind him.*

The chatter of the unseen audience dies away.

Sauveur I can't read, I can't write and I'm no speaker. I'm a journeyman butcher – Citizen Robert Sauveur and I've come straight from the butcheries of Sceaux to this Assembly, not powdered, scented or booted but with the blood of a slaughtered ox still warm on me. I'm here to present a petition for the Ponceau Section. I don't know why I was given this honour. I have no qualifications except if need be, I know how to plough a field, mend a roof and a pair of shoes and I've always earned a living with my hands. But I'm not educated or clever. Yet I'm here on behalf of all sorts and kinds of peoples, water-carriers, caterers, porters, locksmiths, labourers, glaziers, gauze makers and the rest.

But before I can speak for them I must present my credentials. It's important you know what I am. I come from a family of ten or twelve. I'm not sure how many. Most of them died before I was six, of the sweating sickness and starvation. Put all human suffering on one side of the scale and poverty on the other and poverty I think would be heavier. With poverty you are in fear of everyday things like old age, sickness, an increase in the price of bread, a rainstorm that stops you from working, the birth of another child. It's hard to keep a fingerhold on life when the smallest change can make you fall even lower than you are.

All us children had different mothers and I don't remember mine. My father was a butcher and like most, worked, drank and whored quickly through his life. He was spared old age. Strength was all he had. With that gone, he'd've been a bundle of rags, bent double begging outside a church. Instead he died, damned, cursing me. They were deadish times, long winters, short springs.

I started killing when I was thirteen. One livre a day for a twelve hour day, five a.m. to nine p.m. in the summer. I often worked by moonlight, though you don't look up at the

moon much when you're busy. I can't say how high the
moon is from us but it's higher than Notre Dame so it
meant nothing to me. We did most of the butchering in the
streets round Saint-Jacques, Montrouge and Gentilly. There
was always a heavy stink of blood about those places. Blood,
rot and death. We'd chant: 'Now's the time Henri, begin the
knocking. Spread them out upon the floor. Get them ready
for the hammers. Tie them down and let them roar. Keep
them still and then knock 'em. On their marks let them
drop. Keep their heads and feet from piling. Do not let the
killing stop.' Between the slaughterings the men would drink
and huge whores would sit on small stools showing
themselves off to shrieks of laughter.

There were shrieks of another kind from the steers as we
started to slaughter them. They'd be thrown to the ground,
horns tied with rope to a post and we'd smash their skulls
with a mallet. A knife would slit open their throats and
bellies and the blood poured out in torrents which women
caught and made into soup with a few herbs. Then we'd
pull out the entrails and hack the carcass to pieces and hang
it up for sale, still steaming.

Sometimes butchers'd be too drunk to kill the steers with the
first blow and they'd escape smashing down anything in
their path. But the butchers rushing after them were more
dangerous. It was money on the hoof to us and we'd club
down anyone who'd get in our way. I killed two men by
accident like that and three in brawls but they hardly
counted. It happened when we were drunk. We were always
drunk and we thought if things ever change for the better
we'd be even drunker. A friend said to me, 'When the
Revolution comes everything will be wonderful, the Seine
will be brandy.' I said, 'Why not the Mediterranean? If
you're going to believe in something, believe in something
big!' I was right there, but most of the time I was stealing
food from somebody else's plate and dogs would bark at me
in the streets. I lived like the beasts I killed. No difference
except I was full of rage and hate and I didn't know why.

I joined the army and fought in some battles, mostly in mist
and fog. I don't know where or even who the enemy was.

No fame or glory there. I left after a year. It was too tame after Paris. I went back, took up my old trade and old ways.

We didn't understand anything. A man I knew who dealt in horses and leather said he'd been married a year and still hadn't had any children. 'To tell you the truth it's a family sickness. My father didn't have any children either.' he said 'What about you,' I said, 'where were you from?' 'Oh' he said 'I was from his first wife.'

I used to live with a number of women in cheap lodging houses which we'd leave nights without paying the rent, stripping the room and taking the doors and floorboards with us. The first woman I won in a card game and lost the same way. One girl with red hair – I don't even know her name – I bought for a bottle of wine and a salad. She stayed with me for six months and then went missing. Nothing lasts always. She was hooked out of the Seine a week later. I found her one morning, hung up by her feet along the riverbank with the others, wet and dripping – rows of them.

I got another woman that afternoon – that was easy – we slept together dead drunk in the butcheries with a cold carcass for a pillow. But it wasn't the same. I remembered the one in the river and an extraordinary thing happened, I began thinking of her. I'd avoided thinking all my life – what good was it? Yet here I was doing it. Leave my mind alone! Leave it alone! But it was no good. I thought why does she hang there like meat and not others who should be hanging? But the terrible thing about thinking is that it just doesn't stop, does it? It goes on and on. One thought is too many, a thousand aren't enough. Why are there things and not other things? Why is it this way and not that way? I'm a simple man with a small head. I wasn't used to it. It was like having a fever in my mind. I could hardly think, I was doing so much thinking.

Up to then my ears had been as deaf as adders but now I heard voices for the first time, from every hall and open space in the city. There were prophets every day before our eyes, walking up and down the street and they gave dust, and those that were less than dust, a tongue. They began to get hold of me in some kind of way when they spoke of freedom and the Rights of Man. From them I heard that in the beginning there was no rich, no poor, no bondage or servitude, no one person above another. That all came afterwards by violence and cruelty. I learnt that all men and women stood for freedom and only the privileged were ashamed of it and that virtue was an active force, manly and virile. The old world was falling, and through a crack in a closed door I saw a light like two suns and I made discoveries of the truth that had lain hidden in darkness.

Then even the flies used to bite but workers put up with all their miseries, not because they're too stupid to do anything about it but because they're too tired. Day and night, winter and summer, heat and cold, sun and moon, work is woven into the fabric of their lives. That and nothing else. After working the slaughtering street fourteen hours, all we wanted to do was sleep and drink. But now suddenly we had energy to spare. It was everywhere leaping like a living flame from man to man, woman to woman. It consumed us, the zeal and the fire, and we had the strength to turn the world around. Liberty isn't a scrap of paper called legal rights. It isn't being free of something. It's liberty to *do* something, *be* something!

I was there when the National Assembly proposed that there should be less pride, less holding back one with another. No more bowing and scraping and taking off hats. We were no longer to be called Monsieur and Madam but Citizen and Citizeness. Now I was to be a citizen where before I'd been a beast without dignity.

All things changed, even the dress we wore. Before, when they got it too easy and spent it too soft, there was lace and ruffles and silk ribbons and the women wore their hair piled 'hedgehog' style high above their heads, decorated with fruit-bowls and tiny zoos with animals and a small pond. Now our hair is worn natural and we have plain trousers, open shirts, jackets and boots. Small things compared with Europe at war, France in turmoil but the everyday exists alongside the heroic and sometimes is more important to ordinary people like me.

Dress changed, and I changed with it because I felt I could make a difference. I didn't want to be left behind. I had to rise out of the mire in which I lived and make myself worthy of the Revolution which remade me.

I married the widow Fabre. She already had two children and I fathered two more. I have a beautiful etching of us all together made by Citizen Dufois . . . (*He fumbles in his pocket, then stops.*) No, perhaps another time. Yes, another time . . . We live in a large house in the Ponceau Section on the third floor at 130 livres a year for two rooms. If all goes well and my children work perhaps one day we'll move down to the lower floors where the rents are anything up to 700 livres a year, but that's a dream and dreams are never certain.

I'm still a journeyman butcher, slaughtering in the same street my father lived and died. But I don't whore or gamble and only drink a little wine because it is healthy. I do my civic duty now nights, and attend the political meetings of the 'Society of the Friends of Liberty and Humanity' over in the Graville Section. I paid the entry fee of one livre and four sous and now I help pass resolutions and listen to speeches and debates I don't truly understand though I try, I try. But the handbell opening the meeting, the Declaration of the Rights of Man stuck on one wall, the president's chair, the plaster busts of Brutus and William Tell and the hall full of great orators have become part of my life.

And when one of my friends like Jacques the shoemaker reads out by the light of the lamp we bought together, the decrees of the National Assembly and we discuss them and argue and then finish the session by singing Revolutionary songs, I know I belong. This is the way it should be. People like us should never need politicians, we must do the governing ourselves.

To make a man moral you have to make the world he lives in moral too. And that can only happen when there is liberty and justice for all. As for me I'm no cleverer but I'm trying to be honest as this world goes. I know honesty in a man often means he will deceive himself first. I hope that's not the way it is with me. If you can't be good, act it because if you act something you are it. Now I think of my life as a trust to be used for a good purpose and accounted for when it's over, which is why I suppose they call me Robert the Virtuous Butcher. I know it makes my friends smile, especially those that knew me before. I smile too, but I'm not ashamed of the name. Robert the Virtuous Butcher – it has a ring to it.

I'm sure that's why I've been chosen to present this petition for those revolutionaries who are asking for justice from the Revolution. The only question in any crisis is 'what can I do?' When the time came they asked it and acted. Everything else is a waste of energy. The only question, for a sensible man is 'What is to be done?'

You remember, Citizens, the 6th August '93, the Prussian army was breaking through at Verdun? It was only a matter of time before France was defeated and the Revolution crushed. All our best hopes gone down in blood. The Saint-Antoine Section warned this Assembly that the treacherous king must be deposed or suspended by the 9th or the people would take action. On the night of the 9th we did, and the forty-eight Sections from the Roule to the Gobelins formed a commune and the toscin sounded the alarm and the people of Paris marched to the Tuileries and the king's palace. There were thousands of us there that night making sure the Revolution wouldn't die.

We had no leaders. We didn't need leaders and their orders. We'd all heard too many orders – a lifetime of orders. We knew what we had to do without 'em. They called us a mob because of it. But we were no mob, just plain men and women taking destiny in our own hands for a moment. I know, I was one of them and I was surrounded by friends.

When we reached the Tuileries some of the men from Marseilles wanted to talk to the Swiss Guard guarding the palace. They thought they might be able to get them to lay down their arms. We warned them it was dangerous. In the Reveillon riots of '89 the authorities killed hundreds, the rioters not a soul. In the fall of the Bastille we lost one hundred and fifty good men and women, the defendants only seven. In the fight in the Champs de Mars only two loyalists were killed whilst fifty of our people were slaughtered. Violence is authority's weapon and they're not afraid to use it.

But the men from Marseilles wouldn't listen. The Swiss let them in and then opened fire. Three hundred of us died that night in the courtyard, dying like oxen on the hoof. I know, I see beasts die every day. We killed the Swiss later for their treachery and stupidity too, because the king had already gone and they were defending an empty building, bricks and mortar.

Soon after, the king was finally turned out for good and we defeated the Prussian army. The Revolution had been saved that August night. We'd won a great victory. But nothing comes free. Winners suffer as well as losers.

I'm here to speak for the winners. You won't find their names in any book or roll of honour. I'm talking of the men who died or were wounded taking the Tuileries and are now rejected. Men like Pierre Dumont, aged thirty-two, a gauze-maker, who was killed that night and leaves a widow who had received no pension; Antoine Lobjois, aged thirty-nine, a glazier, killed leaving a widow and five children without a pension; Louis de Roy, aged twenty-one, killed at the first gate leaving a mother, wife and two children and denied a pension; Pierre Homelle, aged forty-nine, journeyman watchmaker, lost an eye attacking the courtyard and refused compensation; Henri Bute, aged forty-one, labourer wounded in the leg and refused compensation; Louis Chauvet, aged twenty-four, water-carrier, a hernia scaling the walls and refused compensation.

The maimed will probably die from their wounds one way or another and their families with them. Crippled they can't work and if they can't work they starve. These are men I know. But there are others treated in the same way. I have a list here. (*He pulls out a paper.*) Good men and women, our own people, but officials, civil servants, doctors, remnants of the old gang, have refused to sign certificates of compensation for them in order to save the nation a little money. Civil servants are born with souls like that. But we revolutionaries are not. I know France is at war and every sou must be made to count. But this is a matter of common justice which is why we fought in the first place.

My wife came up to the window in our bedroom this morning and opened it so the air could come in. I could see grass and sky and sunlight everywhere. It seemed an old but beautiful world. And I thought we must cleanse it of all evil, violence and oppression so we and future generations may enjoy it to the full. It'll be a long journey to that new world. We must pick up those who fall on the way and carry them with us.

Citizens, the Revolution can act stupidly because it is human, but never meanly or ignobly, it is too generous and noble a cause. Honest men like Henri Bute and Pierre Homelle are being treated like liars. They aren't liars. But if you don't believe them, believe me. They are honest and brave and they fought and died for us. The Revolution made me and I don't lie. So let us honour our debts, pay what is due to them and move on. We've a whole new world still to make.

III

THE PREACHER

Late afternoon. A priest, **Jacques Roux**, *in a cassock with a dagger stuck in his belt, speaks from a battered pulpit. Behind him, a broken stained-glass window of an angel with a flaming sword. His dog, Georges, lies curled up on the floor beside him, a red, white and blue rosette attached to its collar.*

God created rich people first and then showed them the world they would own and when they came to a field with thousands of headless bodies with torsos and hands like iron, God told them the headless bodies were destined to be poor workers. The rich cried out 'But these heroes with their iron muscles will crush us.' 'Don't be frightened,' answered God. 'I shall place very small heads and brains on their bodies, so until they develop them you've nothing to fear.'

Who're still the oppressors? – the rich. Who're still the oppressed? – the poor. Your slavery is their liberty, your poverty their prosperity. Priests say the poor must be content with their poverty and they'll have heaven hereafter. Idiots, cretinous rag-pickers! My dog, Georges, has more sense. You can have heaven here and hereafter too! You suffer, bleed, die without learning anything. Don't you know whilst you're gazing up at heaven your pockets're being picked clean, eyes plucked out and you're robbed of your birthright, blind to what is done to you?

Christ's priests seized mankind in its cradle and broke the bad news saying 'You shapeless stench. You can never be anything but filth. Your only chance of winning a pardon for being so filthy is if you bow low in perfect humility in the face of all the afflictions, sorrows, and injustices heaped on you. You're poor and you stay poor, that is how it is meant to be. Life is a bitter ordeal. Don't speak out. Just try to save your worthless soul. You won't be able to, but you will give us less trouble by trying. And when the time comes for you to die croaking, the darkness will be as hard to bear as the daylight ever was.' Oh the Church knows its business. It offers fear and punishment, not happiness, certainly not liberty, only servitude, forever and forever.

Religion is a liar and a cheat yet still you hunger for it. That's why you've sent for me, Jacques Roux, Mad Jacques,

Red Roux, Preacher of the Poor, sower of sedition, subverter of all laws, a priest who saw the light of reason and now proclaims fellowship with all who live in dark dens and desolate places. It's fitting I should preach, perhaps, my last sermon in a ruined church in the parish of St Nicholas, summers end.

I go before the tribunal tomorrow, charged with revolutionary excess. Now, I am, it seems, too revolutionary for the Revolution. And so it begins. When power reigned in one man, King Louis, all sorts complained of oppression and the nobility, middle and monied men called on the poor to help. Together we lopped off that top branch of tyranny but the tree still stands and spreads. New branches hid the sun of freedom for the poor, the revolutionary tribunal is one such. I don't recognize its authority to judge me. Only the poor of St Nicholas can do that. I come here to lay the rags and tatters of my life before my peers. Habits are hard to break, Citizens. I come to confess me. Hear my confession.

Do not forgive me Father, for I have not sinned. My own father had twelve children and as I was the cleverest he rid himself of me by sending me to school at the Angoulême Seminary. At fifteen I was ordained a priest when I knew even less about God than I do now. There was a priest on every dunghill, the scummier they were the better they sprouted. But I stayed on and became Professor of Philosophy travelling roads leading from nowhere to nothing, pronouncing without practicing, aspiring without attaining, teaching students to bear with fortitude the misfortunes of others. Like religion, philosophy solves the problems of the past and the future, never the present.

In '79 the Angoulême students rioted over the agony they saw around them and killed a cook by accident. As a suspect teacher with ideas I was arrested and imprisoned, though I had nothing to do with the incident. A month or so later I was released. No trial, no inquiry, authority had decreed it and I had no say in the matter whether I was to be free or in chains. This is how fires are kindled.

Afterwards I spent four years in the Chair of Experimental

Medicine at Angoulême. No more philosophy, endlessly cogitating the universe. But medicine proved equally useless. Physicians know even less than philosophers and priests gangreened together with no cures for the pain of living. They lie, they all lie! Isn't that so Georges? You tell them, I've grown hoarse in the telling.

In '89 I was given this poor parish of St Nicholas and I was born into the real world of starvation and disease and I saw the horror and the hope too. For the Revolution burst over us, smashed the clamps that held us down and swept us up, up with its transforming power. We opened the book we'd never read and on the first page was the word 'Liberty'.

Listen, listen, the Revolution was born in violence. Revolutions must be violent, it's the only way to end the greater violence that keeps the majority of mankind in servitude. Do you think those with privileges would give them up without a fight because you have a charming smile and the best arguments?

Adjuro! Adjuro! I renounced my alliance to Rome and gave it to France. I became a constitutional priest, put off the mitred robes of privilege and put on the white robes of Liberty. No longer a mumbo-jumbo man – into the sewer with the whole breed of moralizing bloodsuckers.

I still practise as priest and physician when called on but not sustained by unjust tithes and church taxes wrenched out of other men's labours. I had to earn an honest living as a pamphleteer and municipal official.

I live with a good woman, widow Petit, born Elizabeth Hubert, once laundress to the rich, now my helpmate, soulmate, who sells my pamphlets two sous a copy. We adopted a son, Emile. A sweet, sweet boy . . . No more of them. Not for your ears or yours or yours. My only fear, Citizens, is not of death but of a life without them. Georges knows. We love them don't we, Georges, eh?

I was elected a member of the Commune and spoke for the poor. I told Robespierre, Saint-Just, Brissot, Hebert and the rest that they could never be the Revolution. Just men and not to be trusted with power. Anyone with authority becomes an oppressor, a parasitic coat of filth on the hide of the common people. Between those who command and those who obey there is only hate. Does it follow that I reject all authority? No, but I always keep my hat on in its presence. In the matter of bread I consult a baker, in the matter of boots, a bootmaker, a house, a builder. For special knowledge I apply to a specialist. But I don't allow the baker, bootmaker or builder to impose their authority over me. I listen to them with the respect they merit – if any – but I keep the right to judge, criticize and censure. Why should we treat politicians of whatever stripe, royal or revolutionary, any different? I listened to King Louis, Mirabeau, La Fayette the same way I listened to the baker and the bootmaker. Don't be fooled by those who set themselves above you. Always look at the bill they are presenting – you have to pay it.

And criticize me too. People thought Citizen Marat and I were enemies because we were ever attacking each other. He called me an extremist, this from a man who declared three hundred thousand heads weren't enough. But we were never enemies, just revolutionaries, doing our duty. Yet neither of us were popular with the legislators. Not my purpose to be popular. I'm here to sting!

To stop me stinging the Assembly hired me to write the report of the King's execution. We didn't do that well. But you'll not squeeze one tear from my eyes over the fate of a royal fool and his followers who talked of honour and died without it. To the boneyard with the whole crew.
(*Singing*.) 'The rich we'll gobble up / Tra lee, tra low, tra lie / With truffles in the rump / And oysters on each eye.'

I love the harp. That's how men and women should die – to the sound of harps – they are so precious. King Louis died to the sound of drums. The Republic had already substituted the Rights of Man for the Divine Right of Kings and Louis as a symbol was already dead. Louis the man was of little importance so why did they make such a fuss about killing him?

We drove through the streets lined with citizens. Give the public what they want and they'll turn out no matter what.

Louis mounted the scaffold in silence. They had three executioners waiting – three! And eighteen drummers! What extravagances just to kill one man.

The knife fell and Louis' head fell with it. The crowd shouted 'Long live the Republic' and then I saw Santerre and the other Revolutionary officials dipping their handkerchiefs in the king's blood. More reactionary relics, splinters from the crumbling cross. What titanic imbecility! Mealy-mouthed lickspittlers to the bottom of their whorish souls.

I wrote it all up in my report but I was the only one who seemed disgusted by the whole spectacle. Invading armies were about to overwhelm Paris, there was civil strife in the Vendee, rebellions in Lyons and Bordeaux and good men and women were dying everywhere defending the Revolution even as the traitorous Louis was dying on the scaffold. But the good and the true had no carriages, no eighteen drummers or three executioners, a Prussian sword in the belly, an English bullet in the chest and falling face down in the mud was their end. That's how ordinary people die, meanly, without harps or even drums to play them out. But Louis, that useless toe-rag of a man, goes in style, his anemic blood gathered up as something precious.

A month later, remember, I led the attack on the Paris food merchants. I'm proud of that action, though those in power condemn me for it, so I know it must've been right. We ask only for food, a home, a little ease, no more crying in the streets 'Bread, bread for God's sake!' But in that bad winter there was nothing but war, famine, and miseries piled on misery. We were at war so we accepted such hardship if they were equally shared. But they weren't. We were dying because of filthy bourgeois graft and greed, the slimy rapacious money-mad exploiters were hording food to raise the price on the open market. Our legislators wrung their hands, threatened in a whisper and did nothing, so women and children starved before our eyes.

Then we flat-bellies marched, smashed stalls, broke into shops and warehouses and found the bread and meat and other foodstuffs they'd hidden in abundance. They asked why we took it and we told them it was because we needed it. Citizen Marat said we should kill every merchant in sight. We made do with a few score strung up in front of their own shops to encourage the others. And it did. Next morning the food markets were filled again with fruit, vegetables, bread and meat. Like Jesus we had performed a miracle of the loaves and fishes.

We must appropriate land and money from the rich who have it in excess and give it to those who need it and live in want. My petitions were thrown out as being too inflammatory but the only way to defend and save the Revolution is by pushing it as far as it will go and then further – and that's never far enough for me.

Then Citizen Marat died, steel through the heart, painless when he had such a painful life. I miss him. No one left to trust. That's why I agreed to become editor of his paper when his staff asked me to keep the bright flame burning. So when those excremental conformists, Robespierre and the Jacobin gang, banned women from political power we took up the cause. They wanted to keep liberty for themselves alone. I wrote that those refugees from the leper house of reaction should be belled and booted head first into the nearest sewer.

In return they persuaded Marat's widow, Catherine, to denounce me to the revolutionary tribunal for besmirching her husband's memory. Poor sweet, Catherine. Grief takes many forms. She wanted to protect her husband's fame and thought I was taking it from him in some way. I shun fame. It always costs too much . . . (*The sun begins to set behind the stained-glass window as a harp is heard playing gently.*)

Late last night I went walking through the streets of Paris with Georges. Just the two of us, Georges padding beside me sniffing every post and doorway and me smoking my pipe – oh there's nothing better – making love perhaps, or making a revolution but with a revolution you have to be right. It was a clear night and empty streets but as we passed St Nicholas Church something strange happened. I was walking but suddenly I couldn't hear my own footsteps, not one, silence . . . I was a dead man walking.

No more of that. (*The harp music stops.*) Tomorrow before the tribunal of mumblers I shall make no attempt to defend myself. That doesn't mean I'll stay silent. Never that. I'll do what I was born to do – attack. If the verdict of that bunch of rotting fish-heads goes against me I die like friend Marat, though struck down by a better hand – my own. (*Gestures to his dagger.*) The Ancients said the good man must walk alone to a right death. You win by losing.

It's been a rich confession after all friends, deserving of some penance, at least five Hail Marys and twenty six Amens. After all I've preached revolution and sedition, slaughtered a king and others, lived in sin and will probably end even deeper in it by killing myself. In the eyes of the Church it is a hundred percent record of failure. But on Judgement Day I expect to stand before my God justified. I do not condemn myself and shall not be condemned.

And so amen (*A glorious sunset behind the stained-glass window begins to illuminate the angel with a sword.*) If it's to be the last amen I go glady. My wife and son will weep, I know and Georges here will howl a little won't you boy? Friends will pause and shake their heads and move on. For they have the difficult part. Living well is so much harder than dying well. They'll remain whilst Mad Jacques Roux will become at worst an obscure footnote in history. I haven't done anything bad enough to be included in the main text.

I've tried to help create a people who are sceptical, rational, critical, not easily fooled or impressed. In a word a free people – ungovernable! It's a dream of course but I've been lucky to have lived through times that made the dream seem possible, when for a moment, we stopped being me and mine, you and yours, us and them, and saw ourselves instead as equals in our common humanity. We are of that generation that so transformed the world that future days and nights can never be the same. We poor, clumsy, men and women turned the world upside down, inside out, round and about. (*The angel with the sword glows in the fiery sunset.*)

One last word from my last sermon. The Revolution isn't complete, hardly begun. Defend it. Don't sit back – act!

Without action no life, without life no perfection, without perfection no eternal peace and freedom. For God is an active power, so we do His work in fighting the great battles, light against darkness, love against selfishness, revolution against reaction, life against death. Come on Georges, it's time for our walk!

Quick fade out as he whistles for Georges.

IV

THE AMAZON

Dressed in a worn nightgown **Théroigne de Méricourt** *sits on a wooden chair in the centre of a bare cell in Salpêtrière Asylum, 1817. There is a solitary window behind her.*

Liberty, Equality, Fraternity, Liberty, Equality, Fraternity, Liberty, Equality, Fraternity, my brain splinters, the words die, rot, or go mad like me, curtains drawn across my face. I ask them for water and a piano-forte and they send me stale bread and second-hand cherries. My head rubbed tight between two cloths, not saying what I think, not thinking what I say and no truth unless it's wrapped in so many lies it can't be found. So I'm sitting in a room where everything stops and the God of Panic grips my throat. What do you expect? You're Théroigne de Méricourt, the one and only and you were devoured bleeding, boneless, with the rest. Revolutions aren't made with rose water and lace fans: d'Herbois deported, Condorcot poisoned, Marat stabbed, Robespierre, Danton and Saint-Just guillotined, Pétions eaten by wild dogs, and I'm not feeling too good myself locked and buried in a madhouse, the smell of fish and dead eyes behind every door. Someone came here years ago to ask me to write my memoirs and I said I hadn't the time, I was too busy being mad. (*Singing.*) 'I, like a ship in storms was tossed / I had to put into land. / Once in port the vessel's lost / My cargo was contraband.' So I end in the jaws that swallowed Jonah, Salpêtrière Asylum 1817, where I hang my heart upon a willow, weeping. Hold. HOLD. I'm sitting but my spirit is still upright, at right-angles to my body, I'm still Théroigne de Méricourt, dead to the world but never weeping.

The wonder is that such things are and others things are not. Some women are born lucky, like blown glass they shatter easy. But I come from peasant stock and the bright stars were dark at my birth so I survive, torn apart by ghosts with webbed feet. (*She takes out a small hand mirror and looks at herself though there is no glass in the frame.*) Look at me now, livid, blotched, and mildew all over. Buried in the dark for twenty years, sick dawns and pale heartbeats. It's natural. Of course there's no mirror in the frame but I don't need one. I know how I look. (*She puts the mirror away.*) Just as I know I was lithe and lovely once. I had Helen's hair and men marvelled at my beauty.

What a sham identity is. Born Anne-Josèphe Terwage on the river Ourthe, forty miles from Liège. Repeat and repeat the story else you'll lose all sense of who you are and what you've done and your life will drift away down and you'll become mad. So repeat and repeat though there are only flickering ghosts who listen out there.

The bird in my head tells me first love is the hardest to forget. (*Singing.*) 'Youth's a season made for joys. / Love is then our duty' . . . He was young and handsome as a crow but what was his name? He was English. I know because we eloped to that green and pleasant land where the whole system only works to sustain privilege and protect status. My lover wanted to give me everything – his money and his name but his family objected and he obeyed like a true Englishman. They always come to heel in the end, born to obey, men with bad teeth, always making washing movements with their hands. They dared not even pity themselves above a whisper.

There are things money can't buy, but in those days, those weren't the things I was interested in, I was dancing a minuet to the music of men and women being tortured. I had other lovers, some lasted at least until breakfast. I think I even had the Prince of Wales, soft in my bed. I did, I did, stale underwear over fat, white, flesh.

Then the Marquis Armand de Parsan fell madly in love with me. There's a word, 'madly'. I was much younger than Armand but I felt old age creeping up on me every night. I sold myself for excitement, travel, two hundred thousand livres with fifty thousand placed out on interest and two bankers, Monsieur Perregaun of Paris and Mr Hammersley of Ranson, Morland and Hammersley of 57 Pall Mall, London. A good bargain I thought then and if I'd've continued in the way of business I would've ended my days in a chateau in Salpêtrière, not a mouldering asylum, eating wet straw. BUT I always went down my own road, let Hell blaze as it pleases. Doors opened and I preferred new errors to old certainties. The quest not the goal. What counts is the action however desperate, what counts is what is missing and never found.

I was combusted, burnt to a cinder, first for money and men, then for music, sovereignty was in me when I sang. (*Singing the aria 'A Change How Deceiving' from Gluck's 'Orphee and Euridice'*) 'A change how deceiving. / Repose I am leaving. / Once more to be grieving. / At life and its pain.'

I had the voice then, gone now, like Armand, who said singing wasn't what he was paying for, oh no. I wanted to be the best so I hired Tenducci, the best teacher in Europe. Friend of Mozart who wrote a piece for him, that should've warned me. Mozart had no morals and Tenducci had no plug-tail – castratos have it hard. He reminded me of that other limp lubcock Robspierre, who also had legs like spaghetti and nothing much between them.

I like men but I don't esteem them. I've been betrayed too often. After Tenducci I was lost and I went in search of myself on the road to Paris and Damascus '89 where I opened my inner eye – the one here in the middle of my forehead. I wasn't blinded like Paul. I saw for the first time the world decoded.

Bang, crash, ahhh, history moved, and burst into flame, the Bastille fell and joy was in the air, abounding and abounding, illuminated by visions, ideas, insurrections, and I was consumed by revolutionary fever, swept up, ebony into gold, suddenly a precipice, white water, rainbows and kingfishers rejoicing and rejoicing. Oh what a storm the light was then, when our evenings touched our mornings!

In ordinary times we don't think the world can be any different from the way it is or ever will be world without end. But at certain moments in our lives when it falls to pieces – a sudden death, an illness, a parting – then the sky splits and the earth heaves up its milk. That's how it was in those early days, balloons rose in us on honeycomb breezes. It was the beginning of the Revolution – before the idea of revolution existed. We uttered one word and altered the rhythm of existence. When I looked up 'Revolution' in the dictionary it was only a word derived from the verb 'to revolve'. We gave it new meaning, we gave everything new meaning.

Men made the Bastille fall but we women made the march
on Versailles. Hunger was the reason, bloated bellies floating
down every alley. I spoke and continued to speak, my inner
flood never failed. 'Where is the bread? – at Versailles!'
'Where are the tyrants? – at Versailles!' Three thousand
women marched that day pistols and pikes, cudgels and
halbards. I rode a black horse in a riding habit of red silk,
red plume on my helmet, pistol and cutlass in my waistband
singing and dancing on the way to Versailles. WRONG. The
fluid passes. Is it smoke I see or has the mist come at last?
Gaps spread and memories cannot furnish the truth. There
was no singing and dancing that day. It was raining and the
women were too weak. I didn't lead the march, I was
already at Versailles when they arrived. But it's a good story
and I believe it.

The King's militia were waiting for us, muskets primed. I
told the women there was one way to make sure they didn't
fire, so we met them with roses in our hair, arms bare, skirts
up, smiling. When men are hard, they are soft. I'd learnt
something from my former life, to carry with me.

The King made promises he didn't keep and Marie-
Antoinette saw me and ran away so fast her hair came down
and she scattered a shower of white powder as she ran.
Later the Châtelet Law Court issued a warrant for my
arrest, and I fled to Marcourt where I was kidnapped by
royalists and carried off to the Kufestein fortress in Austria.
Exciting, isn't it? I'm excited just remembering. All emotions
time-tamed to a whisker now, but my spray-blown days were
so full then, empty now, sucked dry and the world full of
daggers.

The Emperor Leopold charged me with attempting to kill
his idiot sister Marie-Antoinette. I was in prison, locked and
bolted, longing for liberty. Now locked and bolted, longing
for death. Why don't you come? 'I am Death, say goodbye to
the white world. I will cut through to your bones.' Oh yes!
Oh yes!

The Royalist press rejoiced at my capture. Newspapers are
vehicles for the suppression of every generous impulse,
night-carts for tyranny and oppression. The editor Surleau

wrote of my immorality on the sound journalist principle of first besmirching your victim's morals before you destroy them. 'Théroigne is the most terrible of females. Whose inexhaustible paps / Like street taps / Offer drinks for sale / To every passing male.'

The Emperor sent for me to come to Vienna where they all bow from the hips. Despite the trappings of power, Leopold was the kind of man you'd like to have with you when you wanted to be alone. With a little effort he could have been anonymous. But if a slug becomes a king you bow, so I dressed carefully, white robes, hair loose, no powder.

He attacked me for my democratic fanaticism. I said 'You condemn the Republic, that is your duty. I condemn the monarchy, that is mine. I have only one hope, that the principles of the Rights of Man should spread throughout the world. I have a crystal conscience. I didn't try to kill your sister. If I had I would've succeeded.'

The Emperor did not answer. He was a man of few words. He only knew a few and was in truth more interested in my involvement with the Prince of Wales. History after all is only gossip. I told him the Prince took all night to do what some men do all night. He agreed it was his brother-in-law Louis's trouble too. I was freed soon after but I insisted Leopold pay my expenses home. It was only right. I never wanted to go to Vienna did I? Did I?

'Long live Théroigne! Long live Théroigne!' How Paris loved me when I returned. At the Jacobin Club they gave speeches in my honour – the Fair Martyr of France, the First Amazon of Liberty. Oh the energies of '92, the golden glass made manifest, no more walls, the world so big it lost all horizons. Now I stand alone looking out to sea in an old skin that doesn't fit but then life bubbled, boiled and laughed. I was always moving, never tired, reading, writing, making speeches, seeing that there were two fights – for the Rights of Man but for the Rights of Woman too. I thought since men and women are alone they must help each other and so break out of their solitude. Surely it was the moment for woman to emerge from the shameful insignificance in which the IGNORANCE, PRIDE and INJUSTICE of men

had enslaved them? No longer beggars at the feast. I asked
the Cordelier Assembly to give women a consulative vote – a
woman's word flying in the face of history. So they
considered and considered and considered and declared,
though a woman had a soul and intelligence which could be
used for the good of the state, they couldn't give her a vote.
And these, friends, remember, were the best of times, the
best of men. Light the black candles of fear, I felt madness
was upon me even then, the air full of grey flakes falling
softly on my soul.

But I fought in the light of reason. Since all the political
clubs were for men only I formed the Saint Antoine District
Club for Women. Women spent three evenings a week in
reading and discussion and social work and young girls were
taught trades in our workshops. But husbands and lovers
didn't approve. The children were not being looked after,
clothes not mended, dinners not cooked, wives not in their
places. Our leaders naturally agreed, Robespierre who
always wore a corset tightly laced, disliked women, d'Herbois
despised them, Danton used them, only poor Marat had
sympathy for us and he was killed by a woman, dimlaped
down to dust.

At least, when I killed a man it was the right one. I saw the
once mighty newspaper editor, 'paps like taps' Surleau,
seized by the crowd in the courtyard of the Feuillants. I
didn't strangle him with my bare hands. WRONG. It was
more like suicide. We made him eat his own editorials.
Choked on his own venom, killed between his weak jaws,
gasping loudly, spitting blood from his ears. No regrets
there, with one journalist less the world had to be a cleaner,
safer, place.

In the days before the Revolution we couldn't walk through
Paris without covering our shoes with blood from the heads
and hearts split on pikes for stealing bread. And what of
after? When that belly-scratching, short-arsed Corporal
slaughtered millions? No one kept count: numbers sanctify.
Where violence rules only violence wins. It's why I organized
the Women Battalions. We had to learn to drill and fight,
we had so much to defend – the abolition of slavery, full

freedom for Protestants and Jews. And so much more to win. But ringed by fire we had first to destroy the enemies outside. Robespierre preferred the internal ones, closer at hand and they were endless.

Remember, remember that June day with the sun shining outside the National Assembly and hordes of Robespierre's harpies attacking anyone they thought was against their leader. That's me! That's me! 'Citizens, Robespierre is strangling Liberty. Are you free men and women? Will you let this happen?' The female hordes knocked me down and flogged me senseless when I called Robespierre a hairless, half-dead, cod-fish. Ah the women, first they kill poor Marat, then they try to kill me.

They said I was broken by the beating. WRONG. Only heartbroken because I couldn't hear the mermaid singing and was losing words like Liberty, Equality and most precious of all, Fraternity.

Fraternity . . . Oh what a beautiful word that was. When Deputy Lamourette told the Assembly that all our troubles came from one source – our own hatreds and what was needed was more brotherly love, more Fraternity, deputies who had been at each other's throats were on their feet hugging each other, all quarrels forgotten. But it didn't last of course, and men once more talked like men have talked for centuries and so missed each other. I saw demons and the rings of Saturn melt and despair hung from me in clusters.

My brother Joseph had me committed to save me from Robespierre's wrath. I was walled up by the law and by language, walled up alive, a relic of the Revolution, mad in a world where the sane have learned to sneer at words like 'brotherly love' – I know I can see through walls. You live by other standards now and I'm left beached from other times, when we grasped wholes not halves, from all things one thing, from one thing all, and we didn't see ourselves as separate, the leaders and the led.

Like all things the Revolution was doomed to falsehood and decay. We tried to burn away distinctions and bring about a true Fraternity. Failed, fragile as angel-dust in sunlight. The dream dying and the dreamer left bleeding. But we don't lower ourselves by our failures, only by our excuses. We saw one great truth – everything is changeable. All you have to do is stand on your haunches, no longer old trees with knots. (*A bright sunbeam shines through the windows behind her as she suddenly stands up in it, her face transformed in the warm light.*) The Revolution was a radiant city with shining towers and palaces and orchards full of fruit – we saw it! Dust like Carthage now. But twenty years mad in my desert cell, racked and riven by the black, the vision never faded. Twenty years, hard, for a glimpse of Paradise. And I'd pay it again, oh yes, yes, yes, oh yes, yes, yes! The Revolution's crushed, trampled underfoot and the good seed lies buried with me. But one day green shoots will thrust to the sun and stretched before us will be fields and fields of immortal wheat and in those fields those lost words will once more stir my blood and pierce me to the heart, Liberty, Equality, Fraternity! Liberty, Equality, Fraternity! Liberty, Equality, Fraternity! . . .

Lights slowly fade out.

Author's Note

There are so many conditions which are handicapping in the widest sense – being an Arab in Israel, a Jew in Syria, being a woman, gay, black or poor anywhere. These handicaps prevent people making the normal responses to their surroundings, stifle their opportunities and create prejudices in others. Yet we all make sure we suffer disabilities to some degree or other.

These plays, however, deal with handicaps in the more limited sense of mental or physical disabilities such as blindness, deafness, palsy, mental deficiencies; handicaps that are primarily motor, mental or sensory deprivations.

No special sympathy is shown for these disabilities, as that would merely emphasize the differences between the disabled and those without such handicaps, whereas the object is to emphasize the similarities. Acceptance is needed, not sympathy.

It is true that the strengths, weaknesses, loves and hates of a disabled person will often spring from their disabilities. But not always. Someone may be blind but can be a marvellous lover, deaf but handle a complex computer brilliantly, mentally defective but be a good athlete or journalist.

A specific handicap does not imply one specific problem. Some, born disabled, have stable homes. Others come from broken homes and would have difficulties due to their background **despite** their handicap.

Authorities label the disabled as 'the blind', 'the deaf'. It is easier to think of them as part of a group but the disabilities are not always simple in their effect. Within each group there is a whole range of varying responses of how to cope. For a group is made up of individuals, each one absolutely unique. Their similar disabilities do not make them the same. The disabled are not a different species but, like the rest of us, absurd and ridiculous; only they have it harder. They have so much more to overcome. Cripples are the rest of us, dramatized.

Peter Barnes 1989

Nobody Here But Us Chickens was first broadcast by Channel 4 in September 1989 with the following cast:

Nobody Here But Us Chickens

Allsop	Jack Shepherd
Herne	Daniel Massey

More Than a Touch of Zen

Carver	David Suchet
Hills	Nicholas Farrell
Powell	Michael Maloney

Not As Bad As They Seem

Berridge	Stephen Rea
Judith	Janet Suzman
Sefton	Norman Rodway

Produced by Ann Scott
Directed by Peter Barnes

I

NOBODY HERE BUT US CHICKENS

Darkness. The sound of a man crowing 'Cock-a-doodle-do!'
repeatedly.

Dawn light up on a bare, totally white room with a heavy door. A
small table with a plate of sandwiches and clothes over a chair.

George Allsop, *in his underpants, crows and talks urgently to*
himself as the light grows steadily brighter.

Allsop *Cock-a-doodle-do!*, my crowing drives away the night.
Every morning I cock-crow and the day comes again, *cock-a-*
doodle-do! Without my crowing there'd be no light. None at
all. Darkness always. I know to casual eyes I'm just another
farmyard cockerel – an ordinary White Leghorn. I say
ordinary, but of course, one White Leghorn is worth a
dozen Rhode Island Reds, Buff Orpingtons, Jersey Giants or
Grey Dumpies scuttling about, bare rumps dragging in the
dust. We Leghorn Whites are supreme. More popular than
all other breeds combined. Pure Mediterranean – nothing
Asiatic about us. Not a feather or a beak, *cock-a-doodle-do!*
Whites are supreme, *cock-a-doodle-do!* But it's still a
problem . . . I strut like a cockerel. (*He struts around with a*
high-stepping leg action and jerking his neck up and down.) I eat
maize, ground oats, bran and mash like a cockerel, *peck-peck-*
peck. (*He pecks the ground.*) I flap my wings like a cockerel.
(*He flaps his arms.*) And I crow like a cockerel, *cock-a-doodle-*
do! It's obvious I look every inch a cockerel, I do, I do. And
yet they don't believe I am a cockerel. They're convinced
against the evidence of their eyes I'm a man. Yes, a man!
Can you credit it? They have an acute identity problem but
instead of changing themselves they try to change me.
Words like schizophrenic and paranoia are used to weaken
my reason . . . Oh they try, how they try . . . They produce
variations and undulations to harass my brain cells. But I
know what I am, *cluck-cluck-cluck.* I told 'em I lost my body
but not my mind, didn't I? It happened when the wet
creature slid in and a power acted on me. I asked myself the
question 'Who am I?' Am I an obstacle or an opening, a wall
or a door, man or chicken? I'd been with the firm of
Harcourt and Ridley, man and boy, but I slipped out of
orbit; couldn't cope. My story got chopped about somewhere
along the line. Bits and pieces, purges and vivisections, guts

over the sawdust. So I was taken away to rest. What a day! No more whistles and roars from inside. I was in the country walking with trees and grass and so I found myself in the world of the farmyard. I touched peace, at last, in the order of the henhouse, *cluck-cluck-cluck, cock-a-doodle-do*! I saw the top birds pecked all the others and those in the middle ranks pecked those below but respected those above, whilst the fowls at the bottom took it from everybody. This was the England I knew and loved! I was completely at home. So I came out of the closet, wardrobe and coal-hole, no longer ashamed to let everyone know I was a true White Leghorn, *cock-a-doodle-do*! But I'm more than just a rooster. Oh we know that don't we? . . . (*He laughs to himself.*) No Chicken Little me. Even if I am alone I can still only whisper it. Quietly, little puffs, little puffs . . . I'm not really a cockerel, I'm *the* cockerel of myth and legend, the real live rooster booster – I'm Goldcrest, the original Cock of the North! I can't tell those with the white coats and rubber-soled shoes. They'd think I was mad, the pages turning, nutcases together. Instead, I play it canny, and say I'm a common White Leghorn and let it go. They don't believe that so why bother 'em with something that's too big for 'em to grasp. Another secret locked away inside . . . They try to break me, Dora, day after day in this room, but breaking's taking place in rooms and prisons like this all over the world at this very moment – it's all normal, nothing special. That fumed frog of a man, Dr Exley's the worst. But he won't break me, no, not me. We cocks are famous for our courage. Lions are afraid of us, and we frighten away the night and death. They hurt, Dora, oh they hurt, but what's a little suffering? Suffering doesn't matter that much. It happens all the time . . . Dr Exley keeps saying I'm a man like him, as if that's something to be proud of.

I agree I thought I was a man once, mea culpa. I made a mistake, what's their excuse? I know I was only fooling myself then but we can all convert. Towns and cities change their names, I changed my being, blotted out, no roadsigns, not even a station. I won't go back to living a lie. Now I stand newborn, consumed with faith in my chickenness, my rock and my anchor. Let me say it once and for all, loud and clear, in plain English: I'm a *cluck-cluck-cluck, cock-a-*

doodle-do! Nothing could be plainer than that!

There is the sound of a key being turned in the lock. The door opens and **Charles Hern** *strides in dressed in his underpants and carrying his clothes in a neat bundle. He drops them as he sees* **Allsop** *for the first time. The door bangs shut behind him.*

As the two men stare at each other **Allsop** *starts to move cautiously round, with a high stepping action, poking his neck in and out and clucking softly.* **Hern** *continues to stare at him, then moves round in the opposite direction with exactly the same movements. He too clucks softly.* **Allsop** *stops in surprise.*

Hern *makes tiny jumps at him like a fighting cock and starts to crow.* **Allsop** *immediately jumps too and crows. The jumps become higher, faster and fiercer, and the crowing louder. They kick out at each other as they jump. Leaping, kicking and crowing they finally crash straight into each other in mid-air and fall exhausted.*

Allsop *Cock-a . . .!*

Hern *Doodle-do*!

Allsop Steady the Whites.

Hern They're trying to sweat my identity out of me. I don't know you.

Allsop And I don't know you.

Hern That makes two of us.

Allsop You're sailing through the middle of my dream.

Hern I'm not dreaming.

Allsop I am, I can give you the grid reference.

Hern Who are you? What are you?

Allsop I've nothing to hide. I'm a cockerel.

Hern I can see that, pullet-head. What breed?

Allsop Pure White Leghorn.

Hern Commonplace stuff.

Allsop What makes you so special?

Hern I'm a prize Jersey Giant. Basildon Poultry Club. Best of the Best Breed '66, *cock-a-doodle-do!*

Allsop Best breed? You Jersey Giants are all duck-footed, dropped-tail and dropsical.

Hern And you Whites are all lungy and liverish; narrow-necked, canker-combed, dusty-shanked and moulty, *cluck-cluck.*

Allsop This is a restricted area, off limits to all birds, *cluck.*

Hern I didn't fly here because I wanted to. I've a snug henhouse in Basildon. I was forced out.

Allsop They forced me out of my place once, high up on the sixth floor with a view over the gardens. Vermin! Dora took it hard but it didn't worry me.

Hern It didn't worry me.

Allsop Whites're above worrying where they perch for the night. Just so no foxes get near me, I'm all right.

Hern I can see it now. They've set up this meeting hoping the sight of a scraggy rooster like you will drive me out of my mind.

Allsop They could, they're crafty. They try things like that. One hundred and fifty volts and convulsions. Leave your birth certificate on the table and you never see it again.

Hern And the injections. Don't forget the injections.

Allsop With the thirty-foot needles. They try, oh they try.

Hern The more they try the stronger I become. I was a bank teller for twenty years before I found myself. People would come to my window for money. I'd count out five – ten – twenty – fifty – hundred; quick – quick – quick – quick. Two tellers to a cage. Caged birds cramped and grey. Then the light came and I spread my wings.

Allsop Up and away! Top of the dunghill!

Hern Joy and peace, thanks to the great Lord Cockerel Almighty. Oh righteous Father, the world does not know Thee, but I know Thee, *cock-a-doodle-do.*

Allsop I know Thee, I know Thee. But no one accepts it here. They call themselves doctors but they're really white slavers. That's why they wear white coats – it's advertizing.

Hern They're worse than white slavers. Most're into factory farming on the side.

Allsop Save me, Lord, save me!

Hern They try to counter my conversation with drugs, pumping in phenothiazine daily. But religion is my rock, they can't shake my chicken beliefs. I tell them St Catherine was yellow all over and the first Quaker, George Fox, ran barefoot through the winter streets, shouting 'Woe to the bloody city of Lichfield' and Cardinal Richelieu's sister knew she was made of glass and couldn't sit down because she'd crack. So why pick on me? *Cock-a-doodle-do*!

Allsop You fight the unbelievers with words, I do it with silence. I thunder at them silently and when they assault me I enter the silent zone, zilch, where they can't follow and counter their power with the power of silence.

Hern You're deluding yourself. You've got no power. You're just another poor White Leghorn.

Allsop *flaps his arm slowly*. **Hern** *does likewise*.

Allsop You're wrong. Look behind this beak, this comb, these cockerel eyes.

Hern I'm looking.

Allsop It's all fake nooks and crannies, false exits, zigzags, disguises. I've never told this to another living cock before, Jersey, but I'm not just another Leghorn. I'm Goldcrest.

Hern Goldcrest?

Allsop The legendary Cock of the North.

Hern Oh, that Goldcrest. Then this must be the time for revelations. Hang onto your comb and tail-feathers, Whitey, you're the first to know it but I'm no ordinary Jersey Giant either. I'm Chanticleer!

Allsop Who's that?

Hern Chanticleer! Chanticleer! The magical cock from the Roman de Reynart.

Allsop Ah, yes.

Hern I'm the black cock that crowed the night Christ was denied, *cock-a-doodle-do*!

Allsop And I crowed the morn he was born in Bethelem, *cock-a-doodle-do*!

They stop slowly flapping their arms.

Hern We're the Yin and Yan of it, magical roosters.

Allsop Cock heroes.

Hern We must join forces and make sure the liars, cheats and bullies called men, don't win.

Allsop
Hern *Cock-a-doodle-do*!

Allsop Usually two cocks in the same barnyard fight. It happens all over. But there's room for two styles, crawl and breast-stroke. You're a bird of the right plumage. You're no fake.

Hern You have to be on guard every second for fakes. A dubious psychiatrist of my acquaintance dressed up as a chicken to fool me. Dyed his moustache and eyebrows, but I knew. His legs were too thin. And you should've heard his accent. I'm hungry.

He struts around, pecking the air.

Allsop That's a problem in this henhouse. I ask for ordinary chicken meals, maize, sunflower seeds or mash – nothing fancy, but all I'm sent is beef sandwiches. Look there.

Hern You're lucky it isn't chicken sandwiches. We're not cannibals! Not cannibals! Still, beef is quite tasty. (*He picks up a sandwich from the table and eats.*) As I said, you have to be on your guard night and day else they'll trick you. Geese, ducks, fighting bantams, they can really be social workers in disguise, *cluck-cluck*. Why're you staring, Whitey?

Allsop You're eating a beef sandwich!

Hern With mustard.

Allsop Roosters don't eat beef sandwiches.

Hern This rooster does. Needs must.

Allsop You're not even pecking it like a rooster. You're eating it like a man! It's a trick to delude me, the stories drip venom, paranoia lays in wait destroying whole cities and fields. You're one of them in disguise. You're no Chanticleer, no Jersey Giant, no proper cock. You're an agent provocateur!

Hern Feather-legged carbuncle, you're the agent provocateur. Real cockerels are damn smart birds but you're duck-dumb. No true cockerel would believe if he eats like a man, he stops being a cockerel. The Duchess of Macini's favourite cock took tea in the morning on her bed and dined on beef at her table every day. He was still a cockerel, *cock-a-doodle-do*! *Cock-a-doodle-do*! (*He struts around, crowing loudly.*) I can eat a thousand beef sandwiches a day and I'm still the great Chanticleer, a pure Jersey Giant, a real life rooster. But are you, Whitey?

Allsop Of course I am!

Hern You can't prove it.

Allsop Prove it? I don't have to prove it. I don't have to prove anything. No, not me. I am who I am, and I fling my message into the wind. That's the way it is.

Hern Take a good look at yourself.

Allsop I do every morning. My father said I was too ugly, I should grow a beard, but I'm still top of the pile. Cock of the North, *cock-a-doodle-do*!

Hern Better. At least there's a real life crow-note in your crowing. That can't be faked.

Allsop What if there is or there isn't? Crow-notes don't matter. I'm not on approval here, Jersey, pro or con, left or right. You're the one who eats beef sandwiches, not me. Beef, I said beef. It's junk-food!

Hern Beef, pork or salami, outward forms are nothing, Goldcrest, so long as you keep your inner cockerelness. I'm an old bird, as birds go, and that's not far, and I know men lie, cheat and betray – it's in their nature.

Allsop Bullies, liars, blackmailers, wheedlers, toadies, fools who brawl and swagger.

Hern But cunning with it. We fowl can't afford to cling to our animal purity and honour. We must adapt to survive, change with the changing times. If need be take on protective colouring. Though fowl we must behave like chameleons.

He takes **Allsop***'s clothes from the chair and hands them to him. Then he picks up his own clothes and starts putting them on.*

Allsop *Cluck-cluck, cluck-cluck, cluck-cluck.* What are you doing?

Hern Changing with the changing times.

Allsop Those are *clothes*, Chanticleer.

Hern Protective colouring. I'm becoming a chameleon.

Allsop You're becoming a man. It's the first step down the road to sin and degradation. Down, down, down, down.

Hern Have faith. Believe. Do as I do.

Allsop I can't Chanticleer . . . The roof is falling on the world . . . New York . . . Singapore . . . Dartmouth . . . all covered with dust . . . trembling on the edge . . .

Hern Don't be chicken. Believe in yourself. Remember, dressed like a man you'll still be a cockerel. You're still a cockerel. Still a cockerel. Say it – I'm still a cockerel, I'm still a cockerel.

Allsop I'm still a cockerel. I'm still a cockerel.

Trembling **Allsop** *starts to put on his trousers, shirt and jacket.*

Hern A White Leghorn, no less. Never believe because you eat and dress like a man you are one and stop being what you truly are – Goldcrest, the one and only original Cock of the North.

Allsop I am, I am! Yes, I am!

Hern It's not enough for a pure cockerel to behave like a man to become one – oh no, oh no! You can do anything in man's tarred world and still be that rooster booster you magnificently are. So crow you feathered fool, crow. Crow! Crow!

Allsop *Cock-a-doodle-do!*

Hern You hear that outside? You white-coated look-a-likes, there's nobody here but us chickens!

Allsop *Cock-a-doodle-do!*

Hern You're dressed. Do you feel like a man?

Allsop *Cock-a-doodle-do!*

Hern Of course not. Proves my point. Now step out and follow me.

Both fully dressed **Allsop** *follows* **Hern** *round with the familiar high-stepping action, like cockerels.*

Allsop I haven't changed.

Hern You have.

Allsop I'm still a bird.

Hern But smarter, much smarter. You can move in their world without danger.

Allsop I'm camouflaged all over.

Hern You can fake being one of 'em.

Allsop Easy, nothing easier . . . shelling peas . . . rob 'em blind and they wouldn't know . . . Wait, stop the minute hand . . . Why should I? Who should I, would I, want to fake being a man?

Hern Because it's your duty.

Allsop I have no duty except to be what I was born to be – mad as the world says but true to myself.

Hern I've been watching you and I've come to a decision.

I'm recruiting you into the service. I think you're made of
the right stuff, fowl through and through. The Chicken
Brotherhood needs agents like you in the field.

Allsop The Chicken Brotherhood?

Hern First, I must swear you to secrecy.

Allsop I swear. I'll make my scratches on the Official
Secrets Act if you like.

Hern Not necessary. Take your word. The Chicken
Brotherhood is an Intelligence Operation. We must monitor
mankind, Goldcrest. If we don't, we'll be defeated. Look at
Factory Farming. We didn't know the horror of it, couldn't
believe it could happen. But it did. We weren't prepared.
We're fighting it now but it's late. So many millions of our
brethren have suffered and died in agony. What new terrors
could mankind be dreaming up? One day they'll
manufacture synthetic eyes and chickens out of soya beans
and we'll be for the chop. They'll exterminate us like they
did the Great Auk and the American Buffalo. They don't
care, Goldcrest. They don't care.

Allsop I can see the purpose of it but I've never heard of
the Brotherhood.

Hern Good. That proves how successful we've been. We've
tried to keep it very quiet. It has to be all underground,
undercover, underwraps. If they once got wind . . . well you
can guess the rest . . . Kaput.

Allsop Yes, we're cursed and marked down for destruction.

Hern I've been an agent for years. Incognito and then
some. It's a strain I can tell you.

Allsop I know about strain.

Hern Sometimes even experienced operators like me crack
and break cover. They reveal their true identity and start
strutting and crowing. And then they're locked up, double-
bolted and put away. It happened to me. That's why I'm
here.

Allsop I wondered why you were put in with me.

Hern I thought you might wonder. I yearned for the security of a normal henhouse. I found it hard keeping up the pretence of being Charles Hern, Mister. I broke cover last Thursday at a Chinese Restaurant. Chicken Chow Mein, Chicken Chop Suey – it was too much! The menus dripped with the blood of our brethren. I stood up and crowed my defiance.

Allsop Understandable in the circumstances.

Hern Weak. Especially for an experienced operator like me. You'll have to be stronger, Goldcrest.

Allsop Stronger?

Hern By the power invested in me by the Chicken Brotherhood I deputize you Feather Agent Four Five Eight.

Allsop Why me?

Hern Because you're here and not there.

Allsop But what do I do?

Hern Discard your beak and feathers. Act like a man, talk like a man, think like a man.

Allsop It's horrible.

Hern Someone has to do it. Duty, Goldcrest, duty. Once you're mingling amongst them, accepted as a man, keep watch on them and report to me.

Allsop But to go back into their world . . . surrounded night and day by human kind. Never to see any of our own species again. To be completely alone out there. It's more than feathers can stand.

Hern You won't be alone. We've hundreds of thousands of chicken agents in the field. And it's not just us. Other species have their intelligence operators at work too – pigs, foxes, buzzards, vultures and the like.

Allsop Nobody told me.

Hern Didn't know you could be trusted. There's a whole army of animals in disguise and they're working for the overthrow of that evil strain called humanity.

Allsop But how will I know them?

Hern By a certain animal look in the eyes, an animal turn of the head, an unfinished animal gesture. Jackals, hyenas, wolves, behaving like men so well no one can tell them apart. But you will. You'll learn to. You must. It'll keep you sane, knowing there are others like you doing a dirty job because somebody has to do it. But remember, you must never reveal yourself. It's too dangerous. Once started you can't stop pretending to be a man.

Allsop For how long?

Hern As long as it lasts. Your whole life perhaps – or longer.

Allsop Can I do it?

Hern Of course. We're the best. In this whole wide world only chickens can unscramble omelettes.

Allsop How?

Hern By eating them, dummy.

Allsop That's so right.

Hern So you're 'cured' of your so-called delusion, aren't you?

Allsop Absolutely. If I can't fool those emaciated white-coated dwarfs I deserve to be par-boiled and pot-roasted.

Hern They'll think it's a triumph. Because you act like a man they'll believe you're no longer a rooster. It's acting normal that counts with them. They're not interested in what you are inside.

Allsop Inside I'll be a rooster and still they'll preen themselves on their success. But we'll know the truth, *cock-a-doodle-do*!

Hern *Sssshh.*

Allsop Sorry.

Hern No more cocking and doodling, please. You have a higher purpose now.

Allsop That's good. No more drifting here to there at the mercy of the tide. Dora would be proud of me.

Hern Are you ready Mr . . .? What's your given name?

Allsop Allsop.

Hern Mine's Hern. Ready Mr Allsop?

Allsop As I'll ever be Mr Hern.

Hern *bangs on the door.*

Hern We want to talk.

Allsop Open the cage and let us out.

Hern It's Charles Hern.

Allsop And Gerald Allsop. We know who we are!

The sound of a key being turned in the lock and the door swings slowly open and arm-in-arm **Allsop** *and* **Hern** *march out, smiling to themselves as lights fade out to a triumphant 'cock-a-doodle-do!'*

II

MORE THAN A TOUCH OF ZEN

Darkness. The sound of Japanese wood-blocks being banged together.

Lights up on a seedy gymnasium in semi-darkness. Mats on the floor, some chairs in the far corner Left. Sitting sprawled in the shadows, against the side wall Down Left in track-suits are **George Hills** *and* **Douglas Powell.**

The instructor **Joseph Carver** *enters briskly Right, in a Judo outfit, and addresses them from a pool of light, from a solitary skylight.*

Carver Harai-gosphi, O-gosphi knoshi-nage, yoko-goke, wan-kam-setsu, kata-ha-jime Judo is the Path, the Way, the Do, the harmony of circles, efficient use of mind and body, the controlled movement executed with speed, lightness and precision, *aya!* . . . (*He assumes a Judo position, arms straight above his head, right leg bent, left straight out.*) Virabhadrasana One or the First-Warrior Pose. But Judo is more than just a formalized method of combat – it is a way of life. The Judoka is consumed by the cosmic currents. His freedom from fear doesn't spring from his strength or power but from balance and clarity of purpose *aya!* (*He assumes another Judo position, arms stretched out either side of his head, right leg bent, left straight out.*) Virabhadrasano Two or the Second Warrior Pose. There are three basic principles of Judo laid down by the great Kensho Abe. One – all things in the universe're in motion. Two – this motion is flowing. Three – all things flow in harmony. And all this was said by a man only five feet tall. If your balance is right it needs only a little finger to be raised a fraction, a foot to shift an inch and the biggest fall, *aya!* (*He kicks out with his right foot.*) The Ke-Age or the kick to the testicles. Barton Wright developed his own Judo system called Bartitsu, which Sherlock Holmes used to destroy Moriarty. I've developed my own system too, called Bujutsu-Carver. It's Judo sprinkled with T'ai Chi Ch'uan, a smidgeon of Shiatzu – that's Japanese finger pressure for energy, sexual vitality and relief from tension – and more than a touch of Zen: trees have no voice but when the wind blows they sing. Bujutsu-Carver takes the best of the East for the West, *aya!* (*He executes a thrust to the eye.*) The Ryogan Tsuki or Eye-thrust. You can gouge out an eye in a flash with that move. But remember Judo is a spiritual discipline. We reach out beyond ourselves, see the unlit flame, hear sphere music. Heaven's in a single breath, the universe in the movement of a hand. And all for £8.50 a session, plus V.A.T. I've no idea what your backgrounds are but they couldn't be worse than mine. I was born in Chingford and now I'm a Fifth-Dan. Judo is available to all. There can be no barriers here on the Dojo. No barriers in you either physical or mental. The most formidable opponent you'll ever meet on the mat is yourself. But if you have an open mind you'll take everyone and everything in your stride. Now, gentlemen, this will be your first session so we'll concentrate on posture. On your feet and we'll begin a voyage of discovery. But we'd better get some light on the scene and see where we are first.

As **Carver** *crosses to the right wall and switches on the lights,* **Hills** *and* **Powell** *use the wall bars to drag themselves upright, their limbs and torsos shaking violently now that they are moving.*

Carver *turns back to see them twitching and lurching uncontrollably. He stares and deliberately closes his eyes in disbelief. When he opens them again they are still there, still shaking spastically, and trying to stand upright.*

Powell Something wrong Mr Carver?

Carver Wrong? . . . No . . . no, no, no . . . What could be wrong?

Powell Is it because you think we're cripples?

Carver Cripples? Oh I wouldn't put it quite like that.

Powell Spastic paralysis. That's paralysis marked by tonic spasms of the muscles and increased by tendon reflexes.

Carver Ahhh, yes . . .

Hills J-j-judoooo! . . . finger pressure . . . UOKO-gake-wan-ka – soup . . . SHIFT a foot . . . AYA – keee – age . . . pariiii gooooooshi . . . Let's get at it . . . aya-aya-AYYAA.

He nearly falls over in his enthusiasm.

Powell Spastic dysphonia. George suffers from a speech

disorder as well as spastic paralysis – well at least he's not a tenor. It's comforting to know however bad you are you can always find someone worse off than you. Count your blessings, one by one, two by two, eight by eight.

Hills Nooo barriers here on the Dojo-jo-jo-jodo, *aya*!

He attempts the First Warrior Pose and ends up entangled in his own feet.

Carver No barriers but we do have a few technical problems. Nobody told me about you. I could kill Bristow in Admin *aya*! (*He mimes a knife thrust.*) The Tsuki-Koni or Knife-Thrust. (*He breathes in slowly.*) Acki-do . . . acki-do. I breathe in the spirit of acki-do for inner calm . . . Gentlemen, before we actually start you'd better tell me why you want to take up Judo. (*He crosses and picks up two chairs.*) I'm tired of teaching men and women who only want to break bricks with their heads, who have no appreciation of the deeper meaning of martial arts. Will you be able to obtain 'shin' which means heart? Do you have 'ki' which is energy? (*He places the chairs and* **Powell** *and* **Hills** *slump onto them with difficulty.*) Frankly, at first sight, you're not obviously suited to the spiritual disciplines involved.

Hills W-w-weeee're n-n-n-ooot?

Carver No, but that's only at first sight. Tell me something about yourselves.

Powell Handy handicappers – Number 8973 George Hills there and I'm Number 4539 Douglas Powell, Streatham Institute for the Physically Handicapped. I'm an institute man born and bred. I smell of carbolic and quicklime. Years of stone walls, hard beds. But I've been lucky, George here lived soft with his parents till they decided to shuffle off their responsibilities and die. Parents can always be counted on to do that in the end. So he never grew callouses like me. When he joined us he didn't know beans.

Hills Now I'm in an Institute I h-h-have to lick my PLATE clean and p-p-praise the COOK.

Powell You have to learn to surround yourself with yourself to survive. I'm the Institute's Wonder Boy.

M.A.PhD. My fame echoed from one end of Streatham High Street to the other, a distance of some twenty linear feet. Now I write school text books. But I want to develop my body as well as my mind. I always want more. To go to Samarkand as well as stay at home with a family; to sleep alone in a bed and have a woman there too; to have the cherry blossom as well as the timber from the tree; to be famous and unknown.

Hills I want to be a BRAIN-SURGEON.

Carver A brain-surgeon?

Hills I k-k-know I can't be a brain-surgeon, anyone c-c-can see . . . I haven't got the patience.

Carver Ah, no . . .

Hills I'm Judoing because I've had noooo success for sooo long I'm growing UGLY. You need harmony and happiness and circles NOT toooo grow UGLY. A Judok-a-a-a has a clear mind plugged into currents, zzzz, balanced, controlled, LAID-BACK.

In his excitement he topples off his chair.

Powell I'm here because they said I shouldn't, wouldn't, couldn't.

Hills *clambers back into his chair.*

Hills Therapy's no good, they want me too make TABLE-MATS and baskets. I want Bujutsu-Carver.

Powell Not forgetting Zen and Shiatzu up your finger for sexual relief.

Hills But we've both got GET up and GO-GO-GO.

Powell Yes, we'll always have a go, go, go won't we George? Hum 'The Blue Danube'.

Carver Hum?

Powell 'The Blue Danube'

Startled, **Carver** *hums loudly.* **Powell** *grabs* **Hills** *and they attempt a waltz, their arms and legs still shooting out in all* *directions, but vaguely in time to the music.*

Powell Well?

Carver Very impressive. What I was going to say was I don't want you to waste your money. It is £8.50 a week plus V.A.T. and it'll take you at least six months.

Powell To learn Judo?

Carver No, to get you into First Position.

Powell Money can be found. George was left a little and I have something from my books.

Carver Let me be honest. Bujutsu-Carver is just becoming more widely known. I have three former pupils right now teaching the method under licence. It hasn't been easy: part-time jobs and bedsitters in Bayswater, six hours practice every day for years. Sacrifices had to be made. My wife left me and took everything including the pin-cushions. She was married in white you know – what a memory that woman had. Still I can't blame her for leaving, she only ever saw me in Judo positions. That's why I've included Shiatzu sexual finger relief in Bujutsu-Carver. Nobody believed in me then. Even my mother said I'd end up in a Tokyo gutter pissed on by little Japanese dogs. When you're a visionary that's the sort of stupid comment you can expect. Especially from your own mother. But I'll live to see Bujutsu-Carver clubs all over the country; accountants and housewives, bankers and bishops taking an hour off every day to do their Bujutsuing. Stripping away body flab, mind flab. British men and women fit in mind and body – now there's a vision for you. And you two could wreck it.

Hills Hooow? Whaaa soooo SPECIAL about UUUUS?

Carver A year ago I let a Mr Gooms join one of my classes. He was extremely enthusiastic and fit – for a 79 year old. The first exercise he did he broke he broke two ribs. We settled out of court.

Powell We're not 79 and we fall easy like drunks fall. If we didn't we'd be permanently in traction. Our bones're rubbery, not brittle like Mr Goom's.

He throws himself off the chair.

Hills And I'm even better aaat FALLING. I've had more practice. Bones aren't i-i-important.

He falls over the back of the chair.

Carver What is important?

Hills W-W-Whatever we happen t-t-to BE doing at the moment.

Carver A good Zen answer. But gentlemen I can't teach you. I'm only a fourth Dan. You need a sixth or seventh Dan at least. Besides, one breath of scandal, one hint of failure reflects back on Bujutsu-Carver. I've made a desert of my life for it. I can't risk the risk.

Powell You're putting up barriers, Mr Carver. You said the most formidable opponent you could meet was yourself. If you have an open mind you take whatever comes in your stride.

Hills You've juuust got an attack of NERVES – a c-c-crisis of confidence.

Powell Think of the prestige if you pull it off. We'd be the ultimate test of Bujutsu-Carver – a very Everest. You have to tackle us because we're there.

Hills We need y-y-your HELP.

Carver And I need you two like I need a giraffe . . . But, gentlemen, I'm touched – I must be touched to agree to take you on . . . for one session. We'll see how it goes. It's true you are the ultimate test for Bujutsu-Carver to say nothing of Shiatzu and Zen. There'll be more than the sound of one hand clapping if I pull it off.

Hills Whaaa's the sound of ONE hand clapping?

Carver Snow falling, grass growing, dead sparrows; it's soundless sound. Mr Hills, Mr Powell, put your chairs out of the way and we'll start . . . (**Powell** *and* **Hills** *pick up their chairs and immediately bang into each other: disentangling themselves they stagger over to put the chairs down over to the left.*) Zen masters say: 'The Most Valuable thing in the world is

the head of a dead cat.' I don't know what good that is to us
of course. But I'm sure Zen has something to say that is
helpful – if I could just think of it.

*Powell and Hills come back and stand in front of him, their
bodies twitching continuously.*

Carver Hhmm . . . Good posture is the basis of Bujutsu-
Carver.

Hills Gooo posture . . .

Carver Yes, it's the basis of all creative Judo. And the
essence of good posture is the Tanden. The Tanden is a
point, here, two inches below the navel . . . (*He points.*) All
physical movement stems from the Tanden.

Powell Is it Shiatzu sexual finger relief?

Carver No. It just means that if you're aware of your
Tanden you bring your body's centre of gravity down to a
new low. And if your centre of gravity's low it's difficult for
anyone to throw you off-balance. So always think of the
Tanden . . . (*He points to it again.*) Now show me where your
Tandens are.

*Powell and Hills try to point to their Tandens. But, because they
are shaking so, Powell ends up pointing to his chest and Hills to
his groin.*

Carver N-e-a-r-l-y right. Two inches *below* your belly-button
Mr Powell. Up a little Mr Hills.

Hills U-U-Up, up.

They try desperately to point to the right spot.

Carver Awareness of the Tanden is as much psychological
as physical. So concentrate your minds on that point.
Control the mind and the body follows. Hold the Tanden in
your mind. Feel your weight shifting down. Hold the
Tanden . . . Hold . . .

Powell I'm holding.

Hills Tanden . . . T-T-TANDEN . . .

They are now vaguely pointing to the right spot.

Carver Yes . . . Now let's take up a Shizentai posture which is the simple standing position. First breath deeply and regularly . . . Now just stand upright – I know that's difficult but try. Your feet should be about shoulder width apart. (*He takes up the position;* **Powell** *and* **Hills** *imitate him though their feet skid about under them.*) Now the body weight is down to your toes. Knees slightly flexed . . . easy . . . easy.

As **Powell** *and* **Hills** *copy him they find themselves slowly topping forward.*

Hills E-E-Easy.

Carver Now, hands open, fingers curling inwards, wrists flexible, arms at sides ready to grapple, elbows below the level of your hands . . . (**Powell** *and* **Hills** *fling their arms about uncontrollably.*) Head up, eyes alert . . . And you're ready.

Carver *is in the Shizentai position but* **Powell** *and* **Hills** *are twisting themselves into knots trying to imitate him.*

Hills KNEES . . . HANDS . . . fingersss . . . e-e-elbows . . .

Powell Head . . . eyes . . .

Carver It's knees flexed, hands open, fingers curled, elbows low, head up, eyes alert. . . . Hhmm . . . Take a break . . . Well, you could've been worse.

Powell How?

Carver You weren't stiff. No, you weren't stiff. Stiff-armed, stiff-arsed Judo is worse.

He closes his eyes and breathes deeply.

Hills Whaa you doing?

Carver Contemplating non-existence.

Powell Control the mind you said and the body follows, you said. I control my mind. I can pin you to the wall with differential equations. My mind moves with speed and precision – it's a fifth Dan mind. But this body of mine can never be more than half a Daniel.

Carver (*opening his eyes*) And I'm afraid not all the Wisdom of the East, not Zen Masters, Encho Ekai or even Shaku can change a hair of it. I believed with the five-foot nothing Kensho Anbe, that all things flowed in harmony and one candle could light the Universe – Bujutsu-Carver should be a system for all mankind. What good is it if it's only for the fit and the whole? What good is it if some are left outside? What good is it if you can't even Shizentai, can't hold?

Hills Weee can hold onto pain, sickness, loneliness and death – wee're experts of all that. If we didn't HOLD we'd s-s-shake ourselves to pieces. No rest for us, I guess we must be wicked. I wake up EVERY e-e-every morning saying 'Hold. Don't let go.' I let go-o-o once when my PARENTS d-d-died on me. I tried tooo listen to the birds b-b-but they wouldn't put u-u-up with ME. I couldn't look out of the RIGHT window. Sooo I bought a razor to cut my throat. I ended up s-s-slashing my k-k-kneecap instead I was shaking so much. NOW I hold. There's no-one in the world like us handicappers for H-H-HOLDING.

Powell George's right. I was so busy thinking I was forgetting.

Carver Zen Master Joshu always said, 'If you've got nothing on your mind, throw it out. And if you can't throw it out, carry it out.'

Hills Whaa did he mean?

Carver Who knows? Those damn Zen Masters were always saying things like that . . . We'll give it another try. Shizentai . . . But first the Tanden . . . (*He points.*) It's here. Hold it in your mind's eye. And point. Hold and point. (*This time* **Powell**'s *shaking finger points to his thigh and* **Hills**'s *to his right side.*) No . . . No . . . I'll show you exactly.

He moves forward and takes **Hills**'s *hand to direct his waving finger to the correct spot. As he does so* **Hills** *judders convulsively sending* **Carver** *crashing to the floor.*

Powell *and* **Hills** *look down at him in horror.*

Hills Oooh . . .

Powell He didn't mean it, did you George?

Hills Nooooo!

Carver That's the first time I've been off my feet since '68.

Hills I-I-I feel in a p-p-pretty p-p-palsy state. W-W-Weee've BLOWN it, eh Mr Carver?

Carver *Aya!* (*He jumps up and mimes a Judo hold.*) The Gya-ku-juji-jime or Reverse Cross Strangle! I was forgetting the great Zen principle of turning disadvantages to advantage. The famous one-armed fighter Kusunda became a supreme Judo champion because he followed the advice of his Zen teacher and secretly practised Hanemakikomi holds. Now the Hanemakikomi's can only be countered by grabbing your opponent's right arm. But Kusunda didn't have a right arm. By the time his opponents had adjusted to his empty sleeve he'd thrown them.

Powell But we haven't got empty sleeves.

Carver No, you've got the shakes, which is better. I made the mistake of trying to overcome them instead of using 'em. Most Judoka are well-balanced, low-slung, poised fighters. You'll be the opposite – off-balanced, high-strung and a shambles. They won't be expecting that. Good Judo is sneaky. Oh, it's sneaky. You see a Judoka tries to anticipate his opponent's next move. They can sense if it's going to be a hip throw, an ankle sweep or a shoulder wheel. But in your case they won't know your next move because you're moving all the time. Take the simple Shizentai position . . . (*He assumes the position.*) Now you . . . (**Powell** and **Hills** *try to imitate him despite their shaking.*) That's good . . . Now as your opponent I come forward to grab your arms. (*He moves forward to take* **Powell**'s *forearms but keeps missing them because of* **Powell**'s *shaking.*) See, see, it works! Whilst I'm trying to catch hold you could ankle sweep me. (*He finally catches hold of* **Powell** *and finds himself juddering and shaking as well.*) I'm disorientated . . . I've lost my Tanden. You could Seri-nage me or give me the old Hiza-guruma. The possibilities are endless. (*He lets go of* **Powell**.) You'll have to be taught the moves of course. But I can see you as champions.

Hills C-C-Champions? Bujutsu-Carver CHAMPS, sexy finger CHAMPS, heads of dead cats C-C-CHAMPS?

Powell Are you sure we really look like championship material, Mr Carver?

Carver With practice. But all those shakes and twitches. Not good enough gentlemen.

Powell We know.

Carver They're much too small.

Powell Too small?

Carver I want strong shakes, convulsive twitches, titanic lurches.

Hills } W-W-What?
Powell

Carver *imitates* **Powell** *and* **Hills***'s movements violently shaking and flinging out his arms and legs with exaggerated wildness.*

Carver No half-measure, gentlemen. I aim to make spastic paralysis a fighting force to be reckoned with, *aya*! (*He thrusts out his right arm and leg.*) The Ago-Oshi Palsey or the Palsey-Punch to Groin and Throat.

Powell But we've spent our lives trying to shake less.

Carver I want more, not less. You hit the target by aiming in the opposite direction – that's sound Zen. I want bold, full-blooded convulsions . . . (*He jumps and shakes violently.*) You were born to shake, rattle and roll. Don't fight it, go with it. Go, go, go!

Powell But it's different.

Carver Of course it's different. You've got to start thinking like winners.

Hills H-H-HARD. W-W-We've always been LOSERS.

Carver The difference between winners and losers is that winners always expect to win and they do, even when they lose. And remember you'll win not despite your handicaps but because of 'em – that's true Zen, gentlemen.

Hills Up t-t-till now OUR h-h-handicaps haaave generally been a HANDICAP. I-I-I m-m-must s-s-say I like THIS w-w-way better. Whaaa about holding our b-b-belly button TANDENS?

Carver Forget your Tandens and hold your shakes. At all times I want you to have a clear mental picture of how you shake, twitch and shake. It's your biggest asset.

Powell Nobody's ever said that to us before.

Carver Because they're not into Bujutsu-Carver or dead cat Zen – the fools. All you'll ever get from them is sympathy.

Powell *and* **Hills** *shudder in horror.*

Hills S-S-S-S-Sympathy . . . *uggghhh.*

Carver Right, assume the Shizentai position again, gentlemen . . . Wait, I've just thought of a lovely opening gambit. Oh when you're on song, the ideas swarm in like bees to honey. Listen, don't shake for the first few seconds. It'll be a bluff. Your opponents'll think you're just ordinary fighters, then we'll hit 'em with our Spastic Variations . . . Oh, it's so beautifully sneaky . . . Right, into the Shizentai (*The three take up the Shizentai positions, arms out, knees flexed.*) Keep it still . . . (*They are still.*) That's good . . . Now shake it. (*The three shake more wildly than ever before.*) That's good, *ahh!* (*In his eagerness,* **Powell** *has blundered into him and has convulsively brought his knee up into* **Carver**'s *stomach.*) Ooooh-ah!

Powell Sorry!

Carver No, don't apologize. That's good. We'll call it the Hari Hiza Spastic or the Spastic Knee Into the Stomach, *aya!* (*He jerks his right knee up.*) Hold those shakes, men! Hold!

But **Powell** *suddenly stops shaking so violently and looks across at* **Hills** *who also slows down.*

Powell We didn't shake at all just now.

Hills Noooooo, weeee didn't . . .

Carver Because I told you not to. Part of the plan to throw your opponents off balance and keep 'em guessing.

Hills B-B-But weeee didn't SHAKE!

Powell Not once – once, once! Not once! For the first time in my waking life I was at rest.

Hills W-W-We're WINNERS.

Carver Not if you rest. That's not the idea at all. It's just a ploy. We only use it – briefly – at the beginning of a fight. Mustn't overdo it. Anyone can rest. Keeping still isn't important. What's important is getting power into those twitches, shakes and turns. I want every muscle working. No resting, *please* . . . So let's have a full five minutes of shakes. Shizentai and shake it *aya*!

Powell *Aya*!

Hills *Ayaaaa* !

Carver It's all for Bujutsu-Carver. Remember the dead cats. Shake and hold. Now – shake! Shake! Shake!

All three are shaking and twitching furiously as the lights slowly fade out.

III

NOT AS BAD AS THEY SEEM

Lights up on a bedroom. Late afternoon. **Paul Berridge** *and*
Judith Sefton *are in bed. Door Left, window Right.* **Berridge**'s
clothes are placed neatly over the back of a chair nearby. **Judith** *is
smoking a cigarette in bed.*

Berridge My ex-wife never smoked in bed after we made
love. She said one drag was enough. She was kinky, kept
asking me to hurt her. So I told her her budgie was dead.

Judith Harvey was like that too. He said he had marks all
over his body from women touching him with ten-foot poles.
The man was either mad or both. I knew he was a lousy
lover in just eight seconds flat.

Berridge Actually, I've never thought of myself as a great
lover, not since the day they caught a Peeping Tom booing
me.

Judith Rhino horns're supposed to be the best aphrodisiacs
but they have one side-effect – you keep charging Morris
Minors.

They laugh.

Berridge They broke the mould before they made you.
You're funny and you're beautiful.

Judith As what?

Berridge As a system of complex numbers.

Judith To be beautiful you need happiness and fulfilment.
When I was young I had ideas I'll never catch again. Why
do you say I'm beautiful?

Berridge Because I see your shape in the sound of your
voice, because my world isn't quite so dark now.

Judith Paul, if we're going to be lovers we shouldn't get too
personal. We'll only stay together if we stay independent. It's
hard but I'm me because I'm me and you're you because
you're you. But if I'm only me because you're you and
you're only you because I'm me, then I'm not me and you're
not you.

Berridge You're right . . . I had another fight with the

Faculty this morning. That bunch would try switching on a light to see how dark it was. Ernest kept saying 'This is only a suggestion, Paul, but don't let's forget who's making it.' He'll have to go, as Head of the Department he isn't smart enough to be an idiot.

Judith But he is my husband.

Berridge That's no excuse. How did you come to marry a man like that? You're intelligent and he has a room temperature I.Q.

Judith I'm so intelligent I was working as a hotel switchboard operator. Sixty-two hours a week, five hundred calls a day. At the end of an eight-hour session I'd pick up the cords and they'd slide out of my hands. But it's a job where you learn how to judge people just from their vocals.

Berridge So what happened, you got lonely?

Judith Tired. I wanted to grab a handful of cords and pull. Instead I pulled Ernest. I didn't want to end up sleeping alone with a hot-water bottle and blackheads. So I married Ernest though I didn't love him.

Berridge I'm glad. Morals don't bother me much but taste *is* important.

Judith We went to Worthing for our honeymoon. It was so dull there, the tide went out one Sunday and didn't come back.

Berridge Believe it or not, when I was a student I worked in a hotel. As a bar pianist, five thirty to midnight, to pre-recorded applause by professional mourners. Maths and music're close even if it's music to drink by. Customers always wanted to tell me their troubles, as if I hadn't got enough of my own. But I never got friendly. They don't tip if they think you're a friend. I earned good money playing. Being working class my family thought I should make it permanent. But I was lucky. I was bright and I knew what I wanted.

Judith Me too – home, security, money and the respect money brings. Now every morning I sit down and eat my cornflakes. I don't know how many I have, fifteen, sixteen, seventeen – who's counting?

Berridge If you plan, the trajectory is always up. At first I thought I'd teach Economics, be a learned professor of usury and selfishness. But I saw the field was overcrowded. So I switched to Maths. A good choice. I'm a creature of order, first, last and always, obsessed with precision and neatness. I keep my pencils sharp and my passions blunted.

Judith I wish Ernest did. He's too passionate for a man of his weight. It's all hot air and heavy breathing in the Groves of Academia.

Berridge Passion blurs. It's like walking in a high wind. You don't know where you are. I've always stayed clear.

Judith What about your ex-wife?

Berridge Ahh, that was a sudden rush of blood to the, er, head. I can't say I planned that in my waking dreams. Sarah was vain and greedy; she'd eat her cake and yours too. But she was vivid. She was *there* . . . Sorry I'm talking about her. Though a marriage dies letters still come.

Judith The past rots. It should be treated with stain remover. Why did it end?

Berridge I heard the weasel sound of pity in her voice. We threw a last party and when it was over a guest said, 'I'd like to say goodbye to your wife.' I said, 'Who wouldn't?' Neat. The rest was messy and a real waste of energy.

Judith I hope I won't be. I mean at the very least it can't do your career any harm having an affair with the wife of the Departmental Head.

Berridge Provided he doesn't find out.

Judith He'd better not. We're both in safe harbour. If Ernest ever looks like finding out we end it. Much as I'd hate to.

Berridge Why? I know I can imitate falling leaves and tall buildings but why pick me?

Judith You're a good listener and when a woman finds a man who actually listens to her she usually lets him into her bed out of sheer gratitude.

Berridge You're good to listen to. And don't worry about the rest. I'll see you twice a week – Tuesdays and Fridays, three-thirty to six, when Ernest has classes and I haven't. It appeals to my sense of order.

Judith I don't see how he can find out. He's so wrapped up in himself he's quite blind.

They laugh. There is the sound of someone coming into the living room. **Ernest Sefton** *calls.*

Sefton (*off*) Judith! . . . Are you in?!

Judith *and* **Berridge** *'freeze' in horror.*

Judith (*low*) It's . . .

Berridge (*low*) Yes . . .

As **Sefton** *is heard in the living-room,* **Berridge** *leaps out of bed and stumbles forward, putting his hands out in front of him. He feels desperately for support along the edge of the bed to the end. He is blind.*

Berridge (*low*) Clothes? . . .

Judith (*low*) Chair . . .

Berridge (*low*) Where? . . .

Judith (*low*) Left . . .

As she clambers off the bed dragging the blanket off in her panic, **Berridge** *bumps into the chair. He catches it before it topples over, but his clothes and white stick, which we see for the first time, fall in a heap. He goes on his hands and knees to pick them up.*

Judith (*low*) Where are you?!

She has picked up her white stick on the floor behind the dressing table, lurches forward and cannons straight into him. She is blind too.

They quickly disentangle themselves and **Berridge** *puts on his*

*trousers. When he tries to zip them up he finds he has them on back
to front.* **Judith** *frantically helps him on with his shirt but in her
haste rips the front. She suddenly points excitedly, poking a finger
in his eye.*

Berridge (*low*) Arrrx.

Judith (*low*) Shh, he's coming – surround Asia – run for
your lives!

Sefton *is heard approaching the bedroom. As* **Berridge** *scoops up
his things,* **Judith** *grabs her white stick and dives for the bed – and
misses it, landing on the blanket on the floor.*

Undeterred, she jumps back into bed whilst **Berridge** *veers off to
the Right as the door opens and* **Ernest Sefton** *stands in the
doorway. He stares at the dishevelled* **Judith** *who is lying full-
length on the bed, but the wrong way round, and ignores* **Berridge**
who is standing in a torn shirt, trying to hold up his trousers.

Sefton Judith? What're you doing?

Judith (*pretending she was just woken up*) Sleeping . . .

Sefton Sleeping?

Judith I didn't hear you come in.

Sefton Obviously.

He crosses straight to her and trips over the blanket on the floor.

What the devil was that?

*He scrambles around on his hands and knees trying to get his
bearing.* **Sefton** *too is blind.*

Judith It must be my blanket. You *do* need a guide dog.

Sefton It's your fault, Pet. Anything out of place and we
blinders're sure to crash into it.

Judith Sorry. I think I've got a cold coming.

Berridge, *slowly and with extreme care, stuffs his socks and shoes
in his pockets as* **Sefton** *sits on the edge of the bed to talk to*
Judith, *unaware he is actually talking to her feet because she is still
lying the wrong way round.*

Sefton I'm not feeling myself either, Pet. That's why I got Tomlinson to deputize for me. I've been teaching at the Henly School for the blind for eighteen years and it's the first time I've missed a class. I got a blinding migraine then this extraordinary thing happened . . . Judith, I think I'm beginning to see again!

Judith *jerks upright and* **Berridge** *lets go of his trousers in fright.*

Sefton Of course when I say see, I don't mean *see* see. I saw shadows and no shadow is black. So there was light. You've been blind from birth but I was struck blind so I kow what light is. Maybe I've been granted second sight.

As **Judith** *quietly turns round on the bed to face the right way,* **Berridge** *pulls up his trousers and moves to the wall Right, and feels his way along it.*

Sefton I'm hoping against hope, but I shouldn't hope. I must turn a deaf eye to all that. But to see a candle burning, girls bathing, *blue*. To see blue again.

Pressing himself against the wall, **Berridge** *has worked his way round to the bedroom window which flies open and he disappears straight out of it. There is a muffled cry and crash.* **Judith** *and* **Sefton** *turn.*

What was that?

Judith Mice.

Sefton Mice? Mice! You can't fool me Judith. I know what it was. It's that marauding cat you're always protecting – not the Siamese. Siamese have a different cat tread. I've got *ears*. I can hear the sound of walls . . . (*He gets up and crosses to the window.*) The window's open, feel the breeze. (*He stands in front of the window and shouts as* **Berridge**'s *dishevelled head appears outside.*) Damn cat! Get off!

Berridge *flinches.* **Sefton** *slams the window shut on* **Berridge**'s *hands. His face contorts in pain. He opens his mouth to yell but with a heroic effort suppresses it.*

There's something wrong with the catch.

Judith Leave it. You've thought you could see before.

*As **Sefton** crosses to the bed, **Berridge** clambers inside as quietly as he can, blowing on his numbed fingers, and clutching his trousers.*

Sefton All I can tell you is that it wasn't all black. I felt I had the power to bend spoons with my mind.

Judith When I see Dr Palmer about my cold, you'd better come along and have your eyes checked. But right now could you be an angel and get me a glass of milk?

Sefton Certainly, Pet. Colds're *the* worst for blinders. With nose and ears clogged, who can judge distances, people or things? Nothing's what it sounds like, cats're mice, mice men, and everything's micky murky.

He exits, closing the door behind him.

Judith (*low*) Hello? . . .

Berridge (*low*). Hello . . . I thought he'd recognize me by the air I was breathing. I've got to change my trousers.

He sits on the edge of the bed and starts to put his trousers on the right way round.

Judith (*low*) This isn't the time to think about being well dressed! Just grease your shoes and slip away. Did you hear? He might be able to see.

This time he has got his shirt sleeve caught in his trouser zip. He hops about bent double.

Berridge (*low*) Congratulations. I feel like I've got both feet in one sock . . . (*Groaning.*) Oh Lord, lay me in some tacky bit of earth that is forever England. I must look an idiot.

Judith (*low*) How do I know? I can't see. I never could. Ernest had years of sight.

Berridge (*low*) That's why he isn't one of us. We're not people who can't see. We're a different species – we're blind from birth, perfectly adjusted, aristos of the dark . . . I'm lost. How do I get out?

He finally disentangles his shirt from his trousers.

Judith (*low*) The door's thirteen feet four inches directly left, the window ten feet three inches from the end of the bed. Follow my pointed finger.

The door opens and **Sefton** *stands in the doorway with a glass of milk in one hand and his white stick in the other.*

Sefton Judith, I feel there's somebody else.

Berridge *jumps onto the bed and cowers down beside* **Judith.**

Judith Somebody else?

Sefton I have this extraordinary feeling I'm being watched by another pair of eyes.

Judith You're upset. You'll probably imagine all sorts of things.

Sefton *taps his way to the bed.*

Sefton I hope I didn't imagine the light and the shadows. I'm using my stick in case you've left anything else about. Here's your milk.

He holds out the glass of milk for her. She edges over **Berridge,** *half lying on top of him to take it.*

Paul . . .

Berridge *reacts, jerks* **Judith**'*s arm and gets a glass of milk in the face.* **Sefton** *sits on the edge of the bed and chuckles.*

Paul Berridge is responsible for all this. He gave me that blinding migraine and afterwards I saw the light. He'd be furious if he found out. The first time we shook hands I knew he was after my job. Smooth. When he sheds his skin he can send me the rattle . . . (**Berridge** *reacts but* **Judith** *quickly pushes him down.*) Berridge has had it too easy. I've had to fight all the way. Everybody was against me. The authorities always favour teachers blind from birth. Oh don't think I don't know what's going on. I know – everything . . . On top of that if you're born sighted, like me, you can't ever forget it. You carry the sun around in your pocket always. Berridge was lucky he was born stone-blind.

Judith So was I and I don't feel lucky. *You* may be though. You'll see dusks and dawns, tigers, mountains and mirrors. I

don't even know what a dusk or a dawn is. I can't see what I
can't feel. My eyes're at the end of my fingers.

Sefton I don't care about the tigers and the mountains.
What I miss is the moment when you wake up in the
morning and one world disappears and another comes into
being.

Judith You'll be able to see me.

Sefton See myself too for the first time in years. I had a
young face then. I'll be older, but I'm pretty confident I'll be
a fine figure of a man. You can tell by my voice.

Judith I may have angry wrinkles.

Sefton Nonsense. I've felt you all over so I can see you're
beautiful. Kiss, Pet.

He bends over to kiss her. **Berridge** *partly under her reacts,
pitching her forward so she and* **Sefton** *crack heads. Undeterred,*
Sefton *kisses her.* **Berridge** *takes the opportunity to slide off the
other side of the bed and goes into a cupboard by mistake.*

Judith I think I'll get up. We'll go in and have tea.

Judith *sits on the edge of the bed and picks up her white stick as*
Sefton *makes his way out. He suddenly stops as he hears* **Berridge**
come out of the cupboard.

Sefton Judith, there is somebody else. There!

He points with his white stick vaguely in the direction of **Berridge**,
who tries not to breathe.

Judith That's me.

Sefton No, the shadow's moving. Ahha!

*He takes a mighty swipe, misses and the momentum whirls him
round as* **Berridge** *turns to avoid the unseen blow.*

*Though they are now facing in opposite directions, they assume
fencing positions for a moment. Shouting 'En Guarde',* **Sefton**
lunges at the empty air and **Berridge** *parries a non-existant thrust.*
Judith *rushes over to blunder into* **Sefton**'s *stick.*

Ahh! Touche! . . . Plie! . . . (*The two men fence, backs to each other.*) It's a touch of the toledo steels!

Judith Ernest, it's me!

*As **Sefton** stops fighting, **Berridge** tiptoes away, stumbles on his jacket and picks it up.*

Sefton Judith?

Judith What's the matter with you?

Sefton It must be nerves. Today's shaken up my whole nervous system.

I'm going to lie down for a minute.

Judith Will you be all right?

*She crosses to the bed with him whilst **Berridge** finally finds the open door by hitting the door frame.*

Sefton What was that?

Judith I was clearing my throat. Lie down, Pet.

*They are both by the bed as **Berridge** exits and is heard crashing into something in the living room. **Judith** reacts instinctively, clasps her hands over **Sefton**'s ears, pulls his face to her and kisses him.*

*A series of crashes and muffled curses from the living room marks **Berridge**'s progress to the front door as **Judith** continues the kiss. Only after she has heard **Berridge** leave does she finish it and take her hands away from **Sefton**'s ears. He gasps.*

Sefton I've stopped breathing. You smell good.

Judith 'Desire'.

He pulls her onto the bed.

*The front doorbell rings. **Judith** gets up.*

You rest. I'll go.

*She exits into the living-room. **Sefton** takes off his jacket in the fast-fading light.*

Judith *is heard opening and closing the front door.*

Sefton This dark of mine is full of eyes . . . I blame it on these short days and long winter evenings . . . I'll see Dr Palmer, maybe he can help . . . in medicine, where there's money there's hope.

Judith *appears in the doorway with* **Berridge**, *who tries to pose elegantly despite the fact he has no socks, his trousers are half done up, his shirt is out and ripped and his jacket torn. He and* **Judith**, *however, force themselves to speak with exaggerated calm.*

Judith Look who it is, Ernest. I mean, guess who it is?

Sefton Aunt Sarah from Grimsby with the elastic-sided boots.

Judith No, it's Paul Berridge.

Sefton The vultures're gathering already.

Berridge I trust I'm not disturbing you, Ernest. I heard you'd been taken ill. It's so unlike you we all got a little anxious. Is there anything any of us can do?

Sefton Oh no, nothing. This is most thoughtful of you and the others Paul.

Berridge (*low, to* **Judith**) I've lost my keys.

Berridge *drops on his hands and knees and feels the bedroom carpet.*

Judith Yes Paul, most thoughtful.

Sefton How did you know I'd been taken sick?

Berridge *jumps to his feet to answer whilst* **Judith** *goes on her hands and knees to continue the search.*

Berridge Tomlinson. He made it sound as if you were really bad.

Sefton No, I was upset. I thought I saw light.

Berridge Did you?

Sefton Who knows? I've been fooled before. But it shook me up like nothing else could. I'm touched you came to see me Paul, and I'm not a man to say that lightly, am I, Judith?

Judith *springs to her feet to answer and* **Berridge** *goes down to search.*

Judith You say nothing lightly, Ernest.

Berridge *finds his bunch of keys.*

He scrambles up and puts them into **Judith**'s *hand for a second to show he has found them.*

Outside the window the winter light has almost faded.

Sefton Yes, given half a chance people are kind. I sometimes forget blindness brings out the best in others. They know forebearance is typical of the blind as irritability is of the deaf. I think that's why there're comedies about the deaf, none about the blind.

Judith (*low*) Till now.

Berridge Sorry I disturbed you, Ernest. I'll leave you to rest.

Sefton Don't go, and please don't apologize. It's good to discover one's colleagues care a little. And I know by your voice the concern is sincere. We blinders have ways of seeing the truth the rest're blind to.

There is no longer any light from the window. It is completely dark so we cannot see **Sefton, Judith** *or* **Berridge.** *We are now as completely in the dark as they have been all along.*

Judith I used to believe we had new ways of seeing too. I was sure I saw a universe of meaning in the sound of a door slamming shut – bang. I thought I could tell if it was the end of a marriage, a job, a friendship or a life. I had a sixth sense developed to the seventh degree. But now I wonder. Maybe we fool ourselves and we're as much in the dark as those who can see – only we're in a double darkness.

Berridge I always thought I knew what I was doing. My life has an orderly shape. Now look at me . . . I mean, I lost my way and fell, coming here. I was so sure of where I was going.

Sefton We all make mistakes, it's human. I was sure I was being watched just now and heard phantom footsteps.

Berridge Suddenly things conspired against me. I felt betrayed.

Sefton Betrayed? I'm the one who's been betrayed.

He is heard getting up.

Berridge You?!

Judith Who? Who betrayed you?

Sefton Hope.

Judith
Berridge   Ahhh . . .

Sefton I hoped, though I shouldn't've hoped, I was going to see. But the world's gone invisible again.

Berridge The world's a cheat. We can't be certain of anything.

Sefton That's something. We have to find consolation in order to survive: if the text is lousy admire the binding. Look at me. I don't think of the light I lost but the friends I've found, eh Paul. Let me shake your hand . . . Do you know you've got something hanging down in front of you? . . . Here . . .

There is a loud ripping sound.

Berridge I think you've just torn off the sleeve of my jacket.

Sefton It's all right, I've got a spare sleeve I always carry for emergencies.

Judith (*laughing despite herself*) This is a pretty kettle of fish and it's a funny place to keep them. You probably tore it when you fell. You'd better stay for supper and clean up. You must look a sight.

They are heard moving to the door.

Berridge (*laughing*) Lucky no-one here'll ever know, we're as blind as bats.

Sefton (*laughing*) Lucky we're as blind as moles in a mist. You see, things never are as bad as they seem.

Judith Why not?

The door is heard slamming behind them as they exit.